The End of Normal

The End of Normal

Identity in a Biocultural Era

LENNARD J. DAVIS

THE UNIVERSITY OF MICHIGAN PRESS · ANN ARBOR

Published in the United States of America by
The University of Michigan Press
Manufactured in the United States of America
⊗ Printed on acid-free paper

2016   2015   2014   2013   4   3   2   1

A CIP catalog record for this book is available from the British Library.

ISBN 978-0-472-07202-6 (cloth : alk. paper)
ISBN 978-0-472-05202-8 (paper : alk. paper)
ISBN 978-0-472-02965-5 (e-book)

Contents

Preface

Biocultural Identities

The End of Normal attempts to bring together speculations on identity in the early part of the twenty-first century. In our age it is less and less possible to think of human identity, indeed even animal identity, without grounding what we know in the terrain of the biocultural. I use that term, coined by David Morris (with whom I cowrote chapter 9) and promulgated by a number of people including myself, to describe the intersection among the cultural, social, political, technological, medical, and biological. The well of this book resides in issues around the body and the mind in the context of disability and disability studies. I explore sexuality, emotion, psychology, genetics, death, narrative, performance, and a host of other issues through a complex interdisciplinary lens.

My inclination as a writer and thinker often leads me toward being a contrarian, or so I'm told. Consequently, many of the chapters in the book will provoke objections on many fronts, as well as some agreement if I'm either lucky or right. Those who are strong supporters of identity politics and diversity will take offense, I imagine, at the opening chapter of this book. Others who treat depression or are taking medicine to cure their depression will find my opinions on this subject either sadly lacking or just dead wrong. Those in the disability community who are strongly opposed to physician-assisted suicide will find much to dislike in my chapter on the subject. Physicians who daily must perform the act of diagnosis might indeed find problematic my raising questions about the very nature of diagnosis itself, particularly that of affective disorders. Those who are convinced that Freud was a patriarchal sexist will perhaps howl when I suggest that he was one of the first advocates of a liberated view of gender.

As far as I am aware, such contrarian positions do not appear out of sheer perversity. Rather, I think, my being professionally situated between discourses, as my university titles might suggest,[1] leads me to see instinctively and institutionally the other side (or sides) of any discipline. Within one profession, truths are often quite clear. But those truths (almost always temporary, by the way) are less apparent to those in other disciplines. And it is probably true that within any discipline, even accepted truths are only accepted by a certain percentage of those within the area of study. So my ability to, say, apply a filter of disability studies over discussions of race or gender necessarily provides a corrective view, as does bringing the viewpoint of cultural studies, for example, to the study of affective disorders or neuropsychiatry.

Of course the danger of such iconoclasm is that you risk being an amateur in a professional setting—a jack-of-all-trades in a world in which increasing specialization is the rule. For the past few years I've been critiquing some aspects of medicine. To a researcher in that field there is a succinct and ready putdown of my work: "His degree is in English and comparative literature." That academic contrarian pedigree is proof in itself, within certain circles, of the fact that I should have no right to comment on what properly trained people do. It is true enough that my degree is not in medicine, and yet at base I do believe that knowledge is not a franchise and that anyone, with diligent study and research, can broach disciplines that have often erected thick and tall walls to keep out noninitiates. In the realm of science, for example, even experts are only experts in their rather narrow chosen field of study. For them to step back and survey the general practice of science or medicine, they will have to do exactly what I and others do. They will have to learn about other aspects of science or medicine in which they have no particular expertise. In other words, all general statements are hobbled or perhaps supercharged by the fact that they have to go in seriously interdisciplinary directions.

In general, I have been between disciplines and areas of specialization. I like to think that I'm even "between between." That interstitial viewpoint can have its advantages. But, as I have been saying, it can lead to being left out of the shoptalk. On the other hand, I have been heartened that my colleagues in disability studies, for example, have welcomed me into a world that can be parochially defined by a certain physical or mental identity card. I am not a person with disabilities, although I grew up in a Deaf family as a

CODA (child of Deaf adults). As an outsider of sorts to almost all the projects in which I have engaged—from the study of the eighteenth-century British novel to my work on obsessive-compulsive disorder—I've had to both watch my manners and also somewhat paradoxically point out the kind of things that visitors can see and residents often cannot. That combination can make me a sometimes-unpleasant guest at the dinner table.

I see my central work as being perhaps a form of rethinking the truisms of a field. Indeed, this book involves a rethinking of not only the work of others but also what I have taken in the past to be true in my own work. I found my model for this kind of rethinking in the career and work of Sigmund Freud, whose own work on sex and gender I rethink in chapter 8. When one reads through his collected works, the striking thing is the way Freud was always reworking his own ideas, consistently adopting what he felt was accurate but never being unwilling to throw out what proved wrong. So his rejection of his founding theory that neurosis was caused by childhood seduction, while causing a lot of distress to feminists half a century later, was a courageous act in the sense that he had to retailor the whole garment of his work. Likewise, his formulation of the death instinct was a radical departure from his central tenet of the life-striving function of the libido. I have also been inspired by the work of Roland Barthes, who was one of my teachers. Barthes came on the scene as a determined structuralist but moved quite easily in midcareer away from the requirements of structure to some form of poststructuralism, characterized by speculation within order or in ordering of his observant and somewhat random index cards (*fiches*, as he called them).

In that spirit, I begin this book by rethinking my own idea of normality that was the basis for my earlier book *Enforcing Normalcy*. My rethinking leads me to see that normality is no longer the defining term in social organization, as I had posited in my earlier work As I argue, diversity now seems to be doing the work of normal in sorting populations. But of course diversity is very different from normality, and I explore those differences in chapter 1. Chapter 2 continues the ruminating process by thinking again about dismodernism ten years after I coined the term. In that period there have been valid and questionable critiques of the concept, and I am now forced to rarify and elaborate some of my initial claims and assertions. Chapter 3 rethinks identity in a more cultural form—asking if the physical or psychological identity of actors in film or theater should play any role in the selection of a person to play a part in a film, television show, or play. Chapter 4 reconsiders the current attitude toward depression, challenging some major shibboleths in psychiatry but also rethinking how disability studies considers affective disorders, particularly major depressive disorder. Since identity in the twenty-first century is increasingly seen as neuroidentity—that is, our vision of ourselves is encapsulated in the phrase "mind is as brain does"—we are moving from a notion of an independent and self-actualizing human to one in which physiological determinants like the function of neurotransmitters or the nature of neural networks are more important. Insofar as depression is concerned, we haven't really formulated a model in which we can best understand this disorder in the context of disabilities. Chapter 5 reconsiders the way we think of genes, often as fixed-in-stone fatalities in our biological lives. I explore the idea that genes are a form of the prosthetic used to replace other aspects of identity and being. Chapter 6 examines the question of identity by discussing the way that diagnosis functions, as part of the impairment-disability paradigm, in the encounter between doctor and patient. I'm particularly interested in the case of diagnosing psychiatric disorders and the nature of the encounter between two identities—that of the physician and that of the client. In chapter 7 I take on one of the big controversies in disability studies—whether or not physician-assisted suicide should be allowed. I wrote this essay in the aftermath of a rather heated discussion with a few scholars, including the late Paul Longmore, that transpired on the DS-HUM email list. I learned a lot from my interaction with Professor Longmore, and my essay is a considered response to many of the issues he thoughtfully raised. My main argument, fitting into the issue of identity, is how we might want to consider chronically ill, dying patients. Should we see them as people with disabilities and therefore protect them from the abuses of ableism, or should we see them first and foremost as patients at the end of their lives and give them the autonomy they wish? Chapter 8 rethinks Sigmund Freud. Based on a series of seminars I taught at the University of Illinois at Chicago, I have had a chance to reread a lot of Freud, and one of the things that struck me is that our preconceptions of Freud as the founder of modern sexism, with his castration theory and the notion of penis envy, are actually inaccurate. In fact, when reconsidered in the way I do, Freud might be said to be one of the founders of transgender culture and theory.

The remaining chapters outline my (and David Morris's) conception of the biocultural. In chapter 9, we reprint the "biocultures manifesto," a polemic that came out of a three-day visit I made to David Morris's house in Virginia. At that time we edited a special edition of *New Literary History* and wrote the manifesto. Our impetus was to rethink the relationship between the sciences and the humanities, and our conclusion was that for understanding entities like identity, culture, and medicine we need to have an approach that links, not divides, the knowledges produced in what have begun to look like very different methodologies. The final chapter is a consideration about how the biocultural approach might work in education.

Acknowledgments

Chapter 5 first appeared in somewhat different form as "Stumped by Genes: Lingua Gataca, DNA, and Prosthesis," in Marquard Smith and Joanne Morra, eds., *The Prosthetic Impulse: From a Posthuman Present to a Biocultural Future* (Cambridge: MIT Press, 2006), 91–106.

Chapter 6 was published in somewhat different form under the title "The Bioethics of Diagnosis: A Biocultural Critique of Certainty," *Journal of Bioethical Inquiry* 7, no. 2 (2010): 227–35.

Chapter 9 appeared in somewhat longer form as "The Biocultures Manifesto," *New Literary History* 38 (2007): 411–18.

CHAPTER ONE

The End of Normal

I begin with not only a counterintuitive claim but also one, for those famil-iar with my work, that will seem a form of self-heresy. If we are now living in an identity-culture *eschaton* in which people are asking whether we are "beyond identity," then could this development be related in some signifi-cant way to the demise of the concept of "normality"? Is it possible that *normal*, in its largest sense, which has done such heavy lifting in the area of eugenics, scientific racism, ableism, gender bias, homophobia, and so on, is playing itself out and losing its utility as a driving force in culture in general and academic culture in particular? And if *normal* is being decommissioned as a discursive organizer, what replaces it? I will argue that in its place the term *diverse* serves as the new normalizing term. Another way of putting this point, somewhat tautologically, is that *diversity* is the new *normality*.

Before I explain what I mean, I am obliged to lay out for those not fa-miliar with my work what I have asserted in the past. In *Enforcing Normalcy: Disability, Deafness, and the Body* I argued that normalcy was a category that had been and is enforced in our culture. I argued that the rise of the concept of normality was tied to the rise of eugenics, statistics, and certain kinds of scientific claims about the human body, race, gender, class, intelligence, strength, fitness, and morality. I pointed out that the development in the nineteenth century of the concept of the normal person (*l'homme moyen*) by Adolphe Quetelet and of the bell curve by Sir Francis Galton acted as both scientific and a cultural imperatives socializing people to find their comfort zone under the reassuring yet disturbing concept of normality. Ex-tremes would be considered abnormal and therefore undesirable. Galton's genius was to change the bell curve to an ogive in which the extreme right side would flip upward and cease being the area of the abnormal. Rather the fourth or fifth quintile would become the location of very desirable traits—in his case, height, strength, intelligence, and even beauty.[1]

Galton devised the ogive or the notion of quintiles because in actuality he was not promoting normality in the sense of being average—since that could also be another name for mediocrity. Rather, he was promoting eugenic betterment of the human race by encouraging the mating of people who had a kind of enhanced normality—which I have called "hypernormality."

Galton used the concept of the normal curve and normality to camouflage what he actually wanted, which was a bigger, smarter, stronger, more dominant human being that corresponded with the putative traits of the dominant social and political classes in a racialized and sexist society. Seeming to be an ideology of democracy and utilitarianism, the norm actually acted as a rationale for rule by elites. Doing that double work of appearing to maintain democratic ideals while promoting a new kind inequality, the concept of normality held powerful sway for more than 150 years. It has worked very nicely to consolidate the power of nations, institutions, bodies, and cultures over weaker entities, institutions, bodies, and cultures. The mythos of the normal body has created the conditions for the emergence and subjection of the disabled body, the raced body, the gendered body, the classed body, the geriatric body—and so on.

And the idea of normal was an effective rationale for a monocultural society that could define itself as the norm and standard. Immigrants, indigenous peoples, people of color, and foreigners were always going to be abnormal and were "proven" to be so using eugenically oriented biometric tests and measures.

I am not saying all that is over. The replacement of *diverse* for *normal* is a process of uneven development. Nor am I saying this is a bad thing. The idea of diversity has many things to recommend it over the concept of normal. On the surface we are better off abandoning some universal standard for bodies and cultures and acknowledging that there isn't one regnant or ideal body or culture—that all are in play concerning each other and should be equally valued. Diversity is in fact a much more democratic concept than normality since diversity applies to the broad range of the population unlike normality, which of course eschews the abnormal.

But it would be naive to see diversity as without ideological content. Diversity is well suited to the core beliefs of neoliberalism.[2] Neoliberalism is premised on a deregulated global economy that replaces governments with markets and reconfigures the citizen into the consumer. The essence of this transformation of citizen into consumer is that identity is seen as a correlate of markets, and culture becomes lifestyle. One's lifestyle is activated by consumer choice—and this kind of choice becomes the essence of one's identity.[3] If neoliberalism is premised on a culture in which lifestyle and choice predominate, then, as Will Kymlicka writes, "liberals extol the virtue of having a diversity of lifestyles within a culture, so presumably they also endorse the additional diversity which comes from having two or more cultures in the same country."[4] As Manfred B. Steger and Ravi K. Roy note, global power elites, media giants, celebrities, and the like serve as "the advocates of neoliberalism" by saturating "the public discourse with idealized images of a consumerist free-market world."[5]

So while normality was enforced to make people conform to some white, Eurocentric, ableist, developed-world, heterosexual, male notion of normality, diversity imagines a world without a ruling gold standard of embodiment. Indeed, the citizen-consumer under neoliberalism is part of a diverse world that is, however, universally the same as far as consumption is concerned. As Steger and Roy point out, "The underlying assumption here is that markets and consumerist principles are universally applicable because they appeal to all (self-interested) human beings. Not even stark cultural differences should be seen as obstacles in the establishment of a single global free market in goods, services, and capital."[6] Diversity may well be seen as the ideology that opens up consumerist free markets by arguing that we are all the same despite superficial differences like race, class, or gender.

How then, given the ideal of openness concerning diversity—where all are welcomed under the big tent of a diverse nationhood—do disabled bodies fit into this paradigm?

To begin answering this question, let's look to popular culture for some signposts. Walmart and Dove joined forces in an ad campaign called "Campaign for Real Beauty."

The advertisement shows us a diversity of women of color and national origins, a lesbian couple, a somewhat transsexual-looking woman playing basketball, and an older woman, as well as the usual white mother and daughter. All the women are full of life, engaging, but not beautiful by runway standards. They sing these lyrics:

Do your eyes sit wide?
Does your nose go to the side?

Does your elbow have a crinkle?
Do your knees sort of wrinkle?
Does your chest tend to freckle?
Do you have a crooked smile?
Do your eyes sit wide?
Do your ears sort of wiggle?
Does your hair make you giggle?
Does your neck grow long?
Do your hips sing a song?
Do your ears hang low?

A visual on the screen says

Let your beauty sing

The message being promulgated is that there is no normal when it comes to a woman's appearance. Diversity is all. And we can say that the key to the neoliberal subject is that when we visualize such bodies we see them ipso facto as diverse—but within certain constraints, as I will show.

This advertisement, along with many others, including the famous diversity series done by Benetton, reflects a trend to embrace the diversity of the human body within certain kinds of limits set by television and Hollywood, cherry-picking the aspects of diversity that appeal to a regnant paradigm. But while celebrating diverse bodies, the ads nowhere show us women with disabilities, obese, anorectic, depressed, cognitively or affectively disabled.

The concept of diversity currently is rendered operative largely by excluding groups that might be thought of as abject or hypermarginalized. It is difficult to imagine a commercial like the one I've described that would include homeless people, impoverished people, end-stage cancer patients, the comatose, heroin, crack, or methamphetamine addicts. These groups fall into the category of what might be called "bare life," or zoe in Georgio Agamben's terminology.[7] Agamben distinguishes between bios, or life in the polis or political state, and zoe, bare life, which can be killed without sanction but cannot be sacrificed. Zoe is a life defined as not worthy of life, not worth living. For Agamben, though, the project of modernity and postmodernity is an attempt to reclaim zoe to bios, to create a biopolitics that involves technologies of life that recuperate zoe to some kind of political moment. But does diversity do the work of reclaiming zoe? In some serious sense we have to say it does not and cannot. It cannot because its vision of a universal consumer-citizen cannot include these groups, who are at base not consumers and most likely never will be.

This is not to say that there haven't been attempts to include disability in the kind of advertising we are discussing. But when such attempts are made, they generally are unsuccessful—most often using disability as a token diverse category and always making it the kind of disability that is photogenic—usually the looks-forward wheelchair athlete. In a rare case of focusing on a particular disability, Benetton created a campaign using models from the St. Valentine Institute in Ruhpolding, Germany. Most of the images are of children with Down syndrome who are likened to sunflowers. As the publicity for the campaign notes, sunflowers with "their stubborn joy and . . . the docility with which they follow the sun" remind us of the smiles of the children of the Ruhpolding institute. This may be an attempt to include disability, but it is based on "normal" people's benevolent fantasies and not on the terms of disability lived by those children and others like them.

I want to make clear that I do believe it is a good thing that we are moving toward promoting diversity and away from enforcing normalcy. And there is both political and social progress in thinking of humans as diverse rather than normal or abnormal. But, in accepting this change, we should by no means feel that the new model avoids the pitfalls of what Foucault calls "technologies of life." It would be difficult to imagine that "diversity" is so different a concept that it could avoid the larger project of modernity—the creation of docile, compliant bodies. One could argue that there is as much social conditioning, care of and for the body, and subjection of the body involved in this version of imagining the diverse human than in the previous regime. Indeed, it would be naive to assume that any contemporary form of social organization does not carry with it elements of control and categorization no matter how progressive it might seem to us at the time.

If there are elements of social control in the idea of diversity, I would argue we can best see them by looking at how disability fits into or does not fit into the category of diversity. To begin to do this, I want to point to a dichotomy between the kind of subjectivity implied by diversity compared to the subjectivity given to disability. My point here is that the idea of diversity is linked to a postmodern concept of subjectivity as being malleable, mobile, and capable of being placed on a continuum, complex, socially constructed, and with a strong element of free play and choice. In contrast to this mutability, disability is seen as fixed—sharply defined by medical diagnosis and sometimes assigned to an abject position as "a life not worth living" or *zoe*. I will elaborate on this point for the remainder of this chapter, but I want to signal now the end run of this argument, which is that while diversity is the regnant ideology, the older concept of normal still holds sway, but only when it comes to disability, particularly when disabled subjectivity is constructed through medical models. Therefore, the ultimate question I raise is whether diversity can ever encompass disability, which is another way of asking whether diversity can ever encompass abnormality or whether *bios* under neoliberalism can ever encompass *zoe*.

To start discussing this general topic, I want to focus on the way that diverse subjectivity is broadly constructed. As I have noted, in postmodernity we can say about identities within diversity that they are always situated as complex, intersectional, and socially constructed—not as fixed or rigid. In this sense it would seem that the older reign of the "normal" with its simple and rigid notion of a norm could never apply to postmodern identitarian subjectivity.[8]

There are of course identities that concern nationality, religion, and even party affiliation. But the pressing identities in the United States, at least, concern some aspect of embodiment—race/ethnicity, gender, and sexuality. In these areas postmodern thought has therefore eschewed thinking of such bodily categories as tied to an essential self. In the case of race, we use the word *racialized* to account for groups formerly thought of as a belonging to a "race." We now say definitively, based on genetic findings, that "there is no such thing as biological race, but of course there is still racism." Under these conditions, in some sense, we are thinking of race as something complexly social. Yet there is a return to genetics concerning race—which we now call "populations" with specific "genetic ancestry"—as geneticists attempt to construct notions of lines of descent through assemblages of HapMaps and SNPs.[9] Yet no one would dare to say that one population was normal and another was not. Even popular television shows highlighting the DNA tracing of ancestry confound the old ideas of race by showing that Oprah, Skip Gates, and Sally Hemings's children are complexly made up of diverse genetic provenances.

It seems clear that postmodern identities are less bound to an embodied, fixed, assigned self and more to a socially constructed, technologically intervened body, which, as scholars like Victoria Pitts-Taylor have pointed out, one can *choose* to have.[10] In other words, an older model of identity, and one tied to the ideology of "normal," might be considered essentialist and hierarchical, whereas the newer notion of identity appears to be chosen, constructed, and in that sense democratic.

Gender and sexual identities are clearly embodied but now are also seen as equally complex as race. We understand through thinkers like Judith Butler that gender is a performative category. Writers like Judith Halberstam and Leslie Feinberg teach us that gender is on a continuum and that sexual identities need not be tied to a specific kind of body. Queer and transgender studies have shown us that a single notion of normality is a procrustean bed in which no one really sleeps and from which everyone kicks off the covers. Genetics shows us that there are a variety of chromosomal identities that don't fit so easily into the gender binary created under the reign of normality.

By and large, diversity is dependent on the notion of what I have called the "biocultural."[11] By a biocultural body, I want to indicate the complexity of embodied identity. Bodies can be the sum of their biology; the signifying systems in the culture; the historical, social, political surround; the scientific defining points; the symptom pool; the technological add-ons all combined and yet differentiated. As Gilles Deleuze and Felix Guattari point out, the body is perhaps best thought of as a *body without organs*, a machine that produces effects. And more recently, Jasbir Puar has asked us to think of the queer body as a series of assemblages.[12]

In contrast to this roving, complex, and shifting nature of identity that is part of the notion of the diverse, we run into a very different notion of disability. Disabled bodies are, in the current imaginary, constructed as fixed identities. Outside of the hothouse of disability studies and science studies, impairments are commonly seen as abnormal, medically determined, and certainly not socially constructed. This may be because disability is not seen as an identity in the same way as many see race, gender, and other embodied identities. And the reason for that is that disability is largely perceived as a medical problem and not a way of life involving choice.

We may want diversity in all things, but not insofar as medicalized bodies are concerned. It is in this realm that "normal" still applies with force. Most people still want normal cholesterol, blood pressure, and bodily functions.[13] The word most people want to hear from an obstetrician after a birth is that the baby is "normal." No one is advocating a celebration of cancer (although we do celebrate people who are fighting cancer), of chronic illness and debilitating conditions. The area of normal applies not only to physical disabilities but to cognitive and affective disorders as well. The *Diagnostic and Statistical Manual-V* (*DSM-V*) has elaborated a dizzying display of lifestyle illnesses that demand medical treatments to cure and normalize people. Sadness, shyness, obsession, sexual desire, anger, adolescent rebellion, and the like now fall under a bell curve whose extremes become pathologies.

Surgical and pharmaceutical interventions are designed to return normalcy or the appearance of normalcy to aberrant bodies. Short children in the United States are now increasingly given drugs to augment their height, shortness now seen as a hormone deficiency covered by insurance. We don't celebrate crooked teeth; we correct them to their "normal" positions. The point is that tolerance for variation in the medicalized realm is far less flexible and inclusive than it is in the world of race and gender. Only in rare cases, such as the Icarus Project,[14] is something like bipolar depression "celebrated," and only within the inner circle of autists and their parents is there a move to "embrace" autism, in fact calling it a form of "neurodiversity."

Because disability is tied to this medical paradigm, it is seen as a form of the abnormal, or what I might call the "undiverse." I say undiverse because diversity implies celebration and choice. To be disabled, you don't get to choose.[15] You have to be diagnosed, and in many cases you will have an ongoing and very defining relationship with the medical profession. In such a context, disability will not be seen as a lifestyle or an identity, but as a fixed category. In thinking about this situation, we can return to Georgio Agamben, but this time to his discussion of the state of exception. Agamben notices, in a somewhat paradoxical way, that "in order to apply a norm it is ultimately necessary to suspend its application, to produce an exception."[16] In this view, it is not so much that normality has been replaced by diversity, but that normality has been suspended and put in a state of exception. The fact that normality exists for disability, but not for the rest of neoliberal diversity, suggests that disability is the state of exception that undergirds our very idea of diversity. Agamben is using Karl Schmidt's idea of the state of exception to describe how governments have suspended laws, or rendered them inutile by not enforcing them, in order to deal with "extraordinary" circumstances such as the "war on terrorism." While Schmidt might have been thinking of totalitarian governments, Agamben is clearly referring to governments in the neoliberal modality. Nonetheless, I think the idea is applicable to the realm of social organization. In this scenario, the norm is suspended because it is too clearly a sign of sovereignty and power (of the pre-neoliberal order). An ethic of diversity can now fill its place, which seems much more consonant with the aims and goals of democracy, which place emphasis on equality—we are all equal in this diverse world with no one group reigning supreme. But the state of exception so created operates tacitly by a fusion of the old regulatory form of the norm and the new openness of diversity, which means on some level that diversity isn't as open as it purports to be. As Agamben puts this, "the impossible task of welding norm and reality together, and thereby constituting the normal sphere, is carried out by the form of exception, that is to say, by presupposing their nexus."[17]

But it is disability that reveals the state of exception as just that by being continuously connected with the exception to the norm. Disability, seen as a state of abjection or a condition in need of medical repair or cure, is the resistant point in the diversity paradigm. In other words, you can't have a statement like "we are all different, and we celebrate that diversity" without having some suppressed idea of a norm that defines difference in the first place. It seems impossible to have difference without some standard that sets what is different apart from what is not different.

Now one could argue that given time, activism, and education, people will come to see, as we do in disability studies, that disability is an identity, a way of life, not simply a violation of a medical norm. Discussions of functionality may help this process along. Yet I want to argue for what seems like a certain incommensurability between the celebration of diversity and the normalization of disability. For diversity to be able to embrace disability, it will take more than consciousness-raising and political activism, both very important in their own right—it will take an entirely other paradigm shift.

What would that paradigm shift look like? I would argue that in the current moment the identity touted by diversity is always a healthy, able, whole one, one in accordance with technologies of life, lifestyle, and the ability to be represented with acceptably uplifting images. Diversity, given the images displayed in the popular media, is always upbeat, happy, alive, touching, proud, and above all healthy. The images we have of multicultural people holding hands in Benetton ads, of women such as in the Dove ad proudly, happily, celebrating their difference, only reinforce the dichotomy I am discussing. It may be hard to see this, but they are participating in the state of exception that may indeed be reinforcing in different ways the norm, both fighting the norm openly and also enforcing it on the level I am discussing.

Here I want to introduce the idea of multicultural or multiethnic identity into this discussion. When progressives describe a multicultural society, they imagine one in which there is no culture that is better than another. We shouldn't have a hierarchy of cultures. So there is a tension between the idea of a fixed identity, which must then be situated on the grid of better or worse—normal or abnormal—and the postmodern malleable identity, with no judgment of better or worse. That is, under the old logic of "normal" there are groups that are standard and normal and groups that aren't. In the ideology of diversity, all groups are potentially equal. Within the ideology of diversity it isn't better to be Afghani than it is to be Sudanese. It isn't better to be a Christian than a Jew, or a North Korean than a South Korean. One may prefer to be, say, Arab rather than European, but that is because one has a cultural heritage and an identity one knows and likes, not because Semitic bodies or minds are proven scientifically or otherwise to be better than Caucasian ones. The old "scientific" justification for racism is no longer widely or officially accepted.

If identities are, for the most part, no longer fixed, then theoretically one has a choice—to choose one identity over another. I want to highlight this idea of individual "choice" because, as I've been saying, it is a central part of the formation of the neoliberal citizen/consumer. Thus paradoxically we choose iPhones, iPads, Xboxes, fair-trade products, and the like to show off "individuality" within a niche lifestyle market. I say "paradoxically" because of course these are mass-produced items that large groups of people can purchase. Michael A. Peters points out that even "welfare and social well-being are viewed as products of individual choice . . . within a free market economy."[18] Choice is a central mytheme in the neoliberal ideology of freedom and the expression of selfhood through globalized market choices.

The whole idea of this kind of choice for the neoliberal citizen/consumer is that it parallels the idea of voting in a two-party representative democracy such as exists in the United States. The illusion is that there is political choice and the ability to make change, while the reality is that choice is limited, and change is only possible as long as it takes place within the broad outlines of neoliberal capitalism. It is important to understand that the model I'm describing is not that of the duped consumer of mass marketing and media, such as described by the likes of Horkheimer and Adorno. Rather, the more subtle, and perhaps fatal, element in the lifestyle-consumption scenario is that the consumer is buying into a world that he or she both approves of and wishes to be part of with the best possible motives. I cannot go into detail here about how this feedback loop works, but a telling example will be the feelings that many had buying iPhones, iPads, and Mac computers. This was not a forced decision, but one taken with vigor and desire—the desire to be part of a community of like-minded, progressive people who want to make the world a better place, who want to be part of a movement that seems to be hip, cool, and synchronous with many other progressive and positive ideals. Yet these purchases are in no way different from buying any other consumer product and are the result of countless hours of marketing research and locating niche markets. To make this point succinctly, lifestyle choice is one of the central motivators and tenets of neoliberal markets. Disability just doesn't fit into this concept of lifestyle choice.

If we move from purchasable signs of identity to collective group identities, we see that there are both identities one can choose and those for which there is no choice.[19] As I've indicated, disability is not an identity one chooses, but ethnic identity might well be less fixed than disability. It may be hard to leave the ethnicity of one's birth, but it is possible. One can live in the culture into which one was born; one can also choose to leave it. Or one can choose to remain separate or to integrate. But there are certain identities that appear not to have this element of choice. These identities are racialized ones and disabled ones.[20]

It is fairly obvious, for example, that one can be born a Muslim and decide to become a Christian or vice versa. It is possible to be born an Argentinean and to become a US citizen. It is even possible to be born a woman and become a man. It is less obvious that one could be born a black and become a white. It is patently not possible to be born a person with Down syndrome and become someone who does not have Down syndrome (although some cosmetic surgeries to normalize the faces of people with Down syndrome are available, and now drug therapies are being researched to improve cognitive skills). The distinction I am making is between identities one can choose and identities one cannot choose. Multiculturalism, with its devotion to diversity, is happy to embrace identities that maintain the neoliberal tenets of free choice but is less able to absorb those that do not. If we see diversity and identity politics as advocating acceptance of all identities, why is it that disability is often the identity that is left out—not choosable?

I recognize that the multicultural situation is different in Europe than in the United States. In the United States issues around culture are far less important than issues around skin color. The United States was formed along with slavery and the subjugation of the native peoples. Both of these forms of oppression rested on the color of the skin—putatively black, red, and white. The claim to culture was made, but it was made to be self-evident—it was "obvious" that whites of European origin had the superior and advanced culture, whereas blacks and Native Americans had a more "primitive" culture. Because the United States was a hybrid European culture, there was no notion of a monocultural superiority among the various white immigrant groups. And even immigrants considered "black"—like the Irish, the Sicilians, and the Jews—eventually became "white." Now, no one objects to immigrants on the basis of their culture. Even the most prejudiced Americans fail to see a problem with eating Mexican or Middle Eastern food, as they revile Mexican or Arab immigrants.

In Europe, the issue of culture is more prominent, although it may well be an alibi for race. The cultural argument on the right sees the incoming culture as optional and a dilution of the national culture. Immigrants see the host country as a site to establish outposts of their native cultures free from and undisturbed by the prejudices of the host country. Of course in France the issue of the veil is crucially in the news. The immigrants argue that wearing a veil should be a choice a citizen can make, while the proponents of the new law note that the immigrant can "choose" not to wear the veil at school or in public. For either side, the recourse is still to a notion of choice.

In either case, the notion of race or cultural background is seen as a site of change. One can in the neoliberal view leave behind a certain lifestyle and become Europeanized, as many immigrants have done. Or one can "choose" to return to ethnic practices, as many younger people are doing to show solidarity with their "original" ethnic heritage.

Even the seeming fixity of race is declining. And with the idea of race, DNA analysis is breaking down the simple binaries that allow race to thrive, as I mentioned earlier. Now we are thinking of race as something complexly social, but also something that involves various acts of choosing and being chosen. For example, Barack Obama came from a white, American mother and a black Nigerian father—but at some point he had to choose to be black. And popular television shows now tout our ability to find out if Oprah is Bantu or how Skip Gates is descended from a European male line. Racialized identities slide over to become consumer products that one can buy from websites like Ancestry.com or FamilyTree DNA.

Interestingly, the new International Classification of Functioning's notion of functionality that is being used by the World Health Organization is an attempt to reduce the binary thinking involved in the normal/abnormal attribution to disability. The ICF manual is a compendium of biometrics marking the range of motion of the human body, functions of the body and mind, and so on. It allows for very specific notation of ranges of functionality so that there can be a universal checklist of capacities and debilities that in some sense can be separated from broader and cruder designations like "cripple" or "double amputee." If these ICF categories filter down into popular thinking, one will no longer classify disability in the normal/abnormal paradigm, but rather there will be a graded scale of activity, functionality, and participation. In other words, disability will move from the hegemony of normal to the relativity of the postmodern notion of diversity. But the problem will not be in the utility of the scales used, but in the notion that disability is the state of exception that allows diversity to function. In fact, if disability is no longer in the state of exception, then diversity itself may have to alter paradigmatically.

Finally, I would like to interrogate the concept of diversity itself. I would suggest that as an intellectual idea, it does not have much to offer. The ideology of the concept is rather simply put: we are all humans, diverse as we may be. In that sense, although our diversity is a sign of our difference, it is also a sign of our sameness, the sameness of being human. This is a proposition with which few will disagree. There is a built-in contradiction to the idea of diversity in neoliberal ideology, which holds first and foremost each person to be a unique individual. Individualism does not meld easily into the idea of group identity. And yet for neoliberalism it must. In a diverse world, one must be part of a "different" group—ethnic, gendered, raced, sexual. It is considered boring if not limiting, under the diversity aegis, to be part of the nondiverse (usually dominant) group. So diversity demands difference so it can claim sameness. In effect, the paradoxical logic is: we are all different; therefore we are all the same.

The problem with diversity is that it really needs two things to survive as a concept. It needs to imagine a utopia in which difference will disappear, while living in a present that is obsessed with difference. And it needs to suppress everything that confounds that vision. What is suppressed from the imaginary of diversity, a suppression that actually puts neoliberal diversity into play, are various forms of inequality, notably economic inequality, as well as the question of power. The power and wealth difference is nowhere to be found in this neoliberal view of diversity.[21] But what is also suppressed, as I have been saying, is disability—particularly a notion of disability without cure. In this sense disability (along with poverty) represents that which must be suppressed for diversity to survive as a concept. In a more schematic sense, difference must be suppressed to maintain diversity (which ultimately seeks sameness). Thus "we are all different; therefore we are all the same" becomes "we are all the same because we aren't *that* kind of different." "*That* kind of different" would refer to that which cannot be chosen—the intractable, stubborn, resistant, and yet constitutive parts of neoliberal capitalism—*zoe*, bare life, the ethnic other, the abject, the disabled—that which cannot be transmuted into the neoliberal subject of postmodernity.[22]

Ultimately what I am arguing is that disability is an identity that is unlike all the others in that it resists change and cure. It is not chosen, and therefore it is outside of the dominant ethic of choice. It is an atavism representing the remainder of normal at the end of normal. But as such it isn't an anomaly, but rather the capstone that upholds the arch of neoliberal notions of diversity. It is the difference that creates the fantasy of a world in which we are all so diverse that we become the same. As such, paradoxically, it upholds meaning and significance because without difference there can be no meaning. Thus disability is the ultimate modifier of identity, holding identity to its original meaning of being one with oneself. Which after all is the foundation of difference.

CHAPTER TWO

Dismodernism Reconsidered

James Boswell, the eighteenth-century biographer of Samuel Johnson, records a conversation in which he and Johnson "stood talking for some time together of Bishop Berkeley's ingenious sophistry to prove the non-existence of matter, and that everything in the universe is merely ideal. I observed, that though we are satisfied his doctrine is not true, it is impossible to refute it. I never shall forget the alacrity with which Johnson answered, striking his foot with mighty force against a large stone, till he rebounded from it, 'I refute it *thus*.'"[1]

Johnson's refutation of Bishop Berkeley's philosophy has become a famous and oft-told story illustrating the refreshing triumph of activism and common sense over the convoluted head scratching of eggheads. Johnson was a pragmatist, and Berkeley was the eighteenth century's equivalent of a postmodernist who claimed that since our perception of the material world was solely based on our sensory information, we could never ultimately prove that reality existed on its own. Johnson's kicking the stone is not only a gymnastic act of refutation but also an expression of his frustration at Boswell's youthful excitement concerning Berkeley's challenging philosophy and Boswell's claim that a deconstruction of reality could not be easily refuted, if refuted at all.

I mention this story because in my consideration of identity from a disability perspective, in light of the biocultural approach of this book, I conceived the term *dismodernism* in order to provide a connection between postmodernism and disability. The essay in which I did this[2] noted that identity politics had become full of contradictions and thus untenable in a variety of ways. The essay also critiqued some aspects of postmodernism's attitudes toward bodies and minds and said that the postmodern vision of the transgressive body was still very much connected to humanist and Enlightenment notions of the whole, independent, and empowered body. I suggested the term *dismodernism* to uphold a view of identity that remains within the orbit of postmodernism but eschews the fantasy of power and agency associated with the supposedly transgressive body. Instead I proposed that postmodernism could rid itself of this atavism of humanism if it would use disabled bodies and minds as prototypes (if prototypes are possible in postmodernism) that would both assemble and disassemble the regnant fantasies of wholeness and completion. This vision of the completeness of the human body and mind seems to be at odds with postmodernism, but nonetheless it is very much a working concept in postmodernist writing. Therefore, I suggested that a disability studies perspective could help to free postmodernism from these trailing remnants of Enlightenment thinking.

Many people seemed to like the idea of dismodernism and used it in a variety of ways. But there certainly were people who critiqued it from the start. I will review those criticisms, some of which are valid and all of which have caused me to rethink my position on these issues. If I were to group my severest critics and give them a name, I would call them Johnsonians. Like Dr. Johnson they kick the rock of dismodernism in a couple of ways. The first is to say that philosophical arguments aside, there really is a primary and foundational identity called "disabled people" or "people with disabilities" and any arguments about the validity or veracity of that identity are either wrongheaded, needlessly convoluted, or just more casuistic arguing about how many angels can dance on the head of a pin. In other words, these critics kick the rock of identity to show that its existence is not problematic. A second level of critique says, "Look, we know that there are problems with the concept of identity, but it's the only concept we have at the moment. We want to use it in political ways that will assist the fight for the rights of people with disabilities." To me this is merely another way of kicking the rock by stressing the pragmatic and common-sense approach rather than a discussion of abstract ideas. Dr. Johnson would have approved. In my defense, I'm here to argue that neither of these kicks seriously addresses the intellectual and philosophical premises that underlie any discussion of identity.

In 2002, when I wrote that essay, there was a nascent and growing feminist and transgender critique of identity politics in its crudest form. Despite that critique, it was the heyday of such identitarian thinking, and each moment brought along a new identity group that wanted very much to join the ongoing bandwagon. There were some notable exceptions in scholars dissenting from the party line, particularly in the area of race. Judith Butler had suggested in *Gender Trouble* that primary identities are not necessarily the starting point for political struggle. Donna Haraway had suggested "affinity" rather than "identity" as a rallying point. Since those inciting moments, there has been a more nuanced and thoroughgoing critique of identity politics, particularly coming from within transgender and queer circles. The transgender movement has questioned the idea of discrete identities, preferring instead to think of desire and gender as disarticulated from each other and deidentifying one's existence as a function of sexual preference, choice, or orientation, and more as a complex interaction of gender moments and shifting objects of desire. So one thing that galls trannies and people who are polyamorous is the attempt to peg them to a particular binary or a particularity of relationship status. And in terms of queerness, the idea has moved from membership to practices and critiques. You could say that in transgender and queer circles the emphasis has moved from individuals, that is, identities, to viewpoints, tactics, and analyses. In that case, the human as subject is being decentered and replaced by various practices and knowledges. This shift can be illustrated, perhaps, by the following observation. There is a telling difference between the chant "Say it loud! Gay and proud!" (itself echoing the 1960s' "Say it loud! Black and proud!") and the chant "We're here and we're queer!" The former considers that the proper response to identity is pride (in opposition to an oppressor's delegitimating and demeaning that identity). But the latter chant simply states a fact—we are here. There is no implication, aside from the use of the first-person plural, that there is any discrete identity—let alone one to be proud of.

I'm talking about queerness because that movement and intellectual community has come together around the critique of binary identities. I think it behooves disability studies to look carefully here and realize that any simple, unitary identity being defended may hark back nostalgically to the civil rights or early feminist era, but it will not speak to the people who have come of age in the last ten or fifteen years.[3] In other words, if the goal of disability studies and activism is for disability to become an identity like those of people of color, or women, or Asian Americans, and so on, it will surely not grab the next generation of scholars and thinkers because its "me-too" approach seems to be looking backward, like Benjamin's angel of history. Indeed, most of the new theorists are more interested, it seems to me, in the complexity of identity, and as a result we are seeing much more discussion about mixed race, multiethnicity, transnationality, and the like. In a hybrid world, identity is intersectional. Few of us are just one thing.

I want to illustrate this point with a news story. A lawsuit was filed on behalf of three amateur softball athletes who were disqualified when they played in the Gay Softball World Series. They were part of a group of five players brought before a committee that accused them of cheating by claiming to be gay when they were not. The committee interrogated them and then decided that three of the five were not gay. The *New York Times* wrote, "sexual orientation is more complicated than a simple gay-or-straight definition. Experts describe a fuller spectrum of human sexuality, influenced by how a person acts, thinks, and self-identifies at a given time."[4] This broader notion of identity is something beyond a binary, as Suzanna Denuta Walters writes: "The framing of 'gayness' as an issue of nature vs. nurture or destiny vs. choice misses the point about (fluid, chaotic) sexuality and about civil rights."[5] Walters challenges biological determinism about gayness and emphasizes the fluidity and chaos of sexuality. If the media is now discussing this kind of hybridity in identity, a monolithic vision of identity does seem a bit retrograde.

Of course, disability studies is not monolithic, and there are certainly descriptions and theories that allow for complex explanations. In fact, the shift I described in sexual identity, from a unitary identity (gay, lesbian, straight) to a notion of the queering of practices and sites of power, had already occurred in Anglo disability studies, which disarticulated the person from the disabling political structure. So in the UK disability meant, at least at one point, a disabling process that could be applied to a variety of minority and disempowered groups. There are many in disability studies who have shown how representation and political power go hand in hand. Yet for the most part, disability studies has until recently relied on, indeed hoped for, a "simple" identity much like the classic definition of being African American or a woman.

It is this problem I wish to deal with first—the recourse to a monolithic disability identity. When I have called this identity into question, I have been met with two critiques. One strong thread of critique of dismodernism is to say that it is a nice idea but utopian. This "realist" approach presumes that the objecting critic is a sensible, level-headed person and not a naive optimist. It also presumes that the critic has some accurate view of reality along with the ability to predict the future. How is it possible to say that the kind of future I am advocating is not possible unless the objector has some firmer grip on reality than I do? As you can no doubt tell, I believe the realist argument to be deeply ideological rather than simply a form of truth telling.

Another rationale that critiques dismodernism's and postmodernism's doubting of identity categories is one that allows what I am saying to be provisionally true but finds that my saying it is (a) troubling and (b) dangerous. My colleague Carrie Sandahl uses both those words in an excellent essay on disability and performance, finding my "call to generalize the experiences of the disabled body to the social body in general . . . troubling and premature. . . . The main danger I see in Davis' dismodernism is that it proposes to turn into a metaphor, this time for the postmodern condition in general."[6] I have dealt with this type of critique in greater detail elsewhere, but here I will say that if an idea is "troubling," what the user of that word means is "I am troubled," which also means "I am disturbed by what you have said." The net message, while cast in the passive voice, is not that the author is wrong or wrong-headed, but that the reader is upset or disturbed. Interestingly, most reader-critics who are troubled never explain why particularly they are troubled, assuming that if they themselves are troubled, then all people must be. Of course, that assumption is at best a generalization. So if we leave the "troubling" aspect of dismodernism aside and move to the "dangerous," we might raise another issue. When a scholar says that another scholar's insights are "dangerous," what the objecting scholar means is that the idea might be harmful or hurtful or might impede some heuristic agenda that is already in effect or that might become effective if only the troubling, dangerous scholar had not raised the issue in the first place.

The dangerous objection claims authority because it takes on both a moral imperative (I know what is dangerous and what is not) as well as a predictive impulse (I can see into the future, and like Cassandra I see doom and woe). In return, I would assert that no scholar has a corner on morality, nor can any scholar predict the future (which takes us back to my defense of utopianism). I would further assert, perhaps more controversially, that no academic idea that is correct could be dangerous.[7] What I mean is that if an idea is correct, it would be dangerous not to say it or publish it. Would we want our knowledge base limited to what is commonly approved as safe and good? An idea may cause other ideas to adapt and defend themselves, but an idea cannot in and of itself be dangerous. The very concept of academic freedom proves the point I'm making (but also can support the accusation of dangerousness). It may be that to racists, certain facts of biology and genetics are seen as dangerous. It is true that to creationists the idea of evolution is dangerous, and to antiabortionists certain facts of biology are dangerous. But in those cases it is easier to see the ideological basis for their fear of facts than it is for other positionalities.

When Sandahl, for example, employs the troubling and dangerous move, what is it that she fears? First, she justly, from her point of view, fears that the idea of disability identity will be lost, and thus she particularly argues for the effectiveness of disabled performers using their lived experience in performance pieces. Dismodernism would seem to her to propose that the foundation for identities in general should be questioned, if not dismantled. The second thing she fears is that disability might lose its centrality, specificity, and embodiedness if it becomes merely a metaphor for the postmodern condition.

So what is dangerous about dismodernism? According to Sandahl, the prematurity of the call to dismodernism threatens to undermine political gains already achieved and to be achieved. The second danger is that dismodernism's request that human subjectivity be modified by what we have learned about the human in disability studies threatens to make disability a metaphor for the human or postmodern condition. I think there is a valid point in the notion that metaphorization can be problematic in terms of identity because it disembodies disability and makes it a template for something else. Others and I have pointed this out before. But I think Sandahl misunderstands my call for including disability insights in the definition of the human. I would be guilty of metaphorizing if I had said, "we are all disabled, in this sense." And in the essay I specifically say I don't mean this. In fact, if anything, I could be accused of calling for metaphorizing normality by saying that disability is normal, that is, normally occurring in the human species, as are interdependence, variation, and incompleteness.

It could also be said that by saying I want to bring disability into the concept of the human, I remain a humanist. While I believe my critique to be antihumanist, as I've said, I do use the word *human*. Perhaps I would be better off saying that a new conception of being (whether human, animal, or elements in the ecology of the planet) could be generated that would take disability into account. What would it mean to say that the environment was disabled by climate change, that animals were disabled by factory farming, as well as saying that humans are disabled by ableism? In some sense this extension of disability might well be seen as continuing the metaphorization of disability, but by another lens it could be seen as expanding the notion of disability to be applicable to a range of states of being beyond simply that of the human body.

Aside from the dangerous-idea/utopian critique, I think one of the strongest arguments against dismodernism comes from the group of scholars calling themselves post-positivist realists (hereafter referred to as PPRs). Sandahl acknowledges them approvingly in her essay as alternatives to dismodernism. These scholars include Satya Mohanty, Paula Moya, Michael Hames-Garcia, and Linda Alcoff, who are some of PPR's best-known articulators. Their central message concerning identity is that postmodernism's view that identity is purely socially constructed is too extreme. Likewise, the postmodernist view that the objectivity advocated by positivism is ideological and also socially constructed is also seen as misguided. These critics generally don't, however, kick the rock since they know and use the theory that is post-positivist, and they acknowledge and have read some of the validity of postmodern theory. In effect, they sketch out a middle ground between the extremes of those who say objectivity is impossible and those who see objectivity as the gold standard of science and other realms of knowledge.

Post-positivist realists, in regard to identity, argue that one's identity is "real" in the sense that people perceive themselves as really of their identity, and others perceive them as of that identity. In other words, in the world of social relations, identity is real and objectively so. The point of PPRs is that identity has validity, and there are better and worse explanations and descriptions of the world of identity. One way to know whether an explanation of an identity is a good one is to talk about the nature of error in any analysis. While it may be hard to describe objectivity, it is easier to describe error. And we can discuss, according to PPRs, the kinds of error present in an argument and ultimately achieve a better description of an argument about identity than we had before.

While not a PPR, Tobin Siebers has found their theories useful. In his brilliant book *Disability Theory* Siebers argues that disability is a palpable identity, palpable in the sense that the lived experience of being disabled is something you can feel, along with physical pain, discomfort, and so on. I will discuss Siebers's interventions in a moment.

For now, I want to discuss my general attitude toward PPR (and I want to make clear that I don't regard Siebers as being an adherent of PPR or even much of a fellow traveler). I am sympathetic to the project of PPR in its sense of forging workable explanations that can further social justice and a progressive agenda. However, I see areas with which I can seriously contend. Although it may seem a form of nit-picking, I would say it is important to consider that for the most part, the PPR argument has not caught on. Google's Ngram shows its appearance as a term emerging in the early twenty-first century and peaking in 2003, declining thereafter.[8] In its early days, there was a headiness about the applicability of the position that was being advocated. But after ten years, there has been little uptake by the academic community, let alone the general public. I don't take lack of distribution to imply that fashionable ideas are the only ones that are right, but I do think that when an approach proliferates in a particular time in history, it has a certain saliency that unpopular ideas cannot have. In fact, the group of scholars involved in PPR rarely use that term, employing *minority studies* instead. But I would say that the tepid response to PPR comes from the fact that the stance it advocates is very qualified and careful, which means that it can come across as wishy-washy and difficult to fit into a sound bite. But it may well be that the lack of response can also be seen as a recognition that the central arguments themselves are not strong ones.

The central point of PPR, for the purposes of disability studies, is that even though an identity may be socially constructed, that construction has a reality as well. Mohanty attacks postmodernism for its insistence that there is no "there" there. If there is no "there," then how can you fight for social justice, and how can you analyze with any certainty things like racism or ageism? The problem is that for Mohanty and others postmodernism is a kind of caricature. I don't think there are many postmodernists who claim that their method is such that it has no applicability.

Let me give an example that might elucidate this point. From the PPR point of view, a postmodern claim that money is socially constructed might be interpreted to mean that postmodernists don't think money is real. But it is entirely possible that a postmodernist could believe that something is both socially constructed and real. For example, the dollar is socially constructed, yet it is nonetheless real. It may have been at one time that money could be exchanged for silver or gold; however, now it is a symbol or a metaphor for those things. We all "agree" in a social way to accept paper money as a form of exchange, and we also "agree" on the price or the value of that money. Stanley Fish has written in this way about the game of baseball as both socially constructed and obviously real as well.[9] Yet the PPRs would have it that the postmoderns think everything is socially constructed, and therefore they don't think that things are real. But that argument itself is a parody of what postmodernism is about. Every postmodernist agrees to use money, and many watch baseball, and although they may object to many things about the economic system, none would say that money isn't real, that it doesn't have real effects in the world, or that they refuse to cheer when Derek Jeter hits a home run. Could it be that PPR has weakened its argument by hammering away at some straw person called a postmodernist?

Now I will return to Siebers's vision of identity. Siebers does not criticize dismodernism per se. In fact, he seems to agree with much of what I describe the goal of dismodernism to be. Yet the direction that Siebers gives to the subject is that he believes that disability identity should be considered real and not simply a construction. He is interested more in the way that social construction happens than in any given theory. In response to a question I asked him at a recent public lecture, he said that he was interested in the blueprint for the way identity is socially constructed, rather than a vague and general statement that identities are socially constructed. He also echoes my point about dismodernism that the error postmodernism makes is that the body is seen as whole and complete. He writes that "the body posited by social constructionism is a body built for pleasure, a body infinitely teachable and adaptable."[10]

For Siebers, pain is real. It's the rock that Johnson kicks. You can talk about a socially constructed, infinitely malleable body that is transgressive and full of *jouissance*, but when it comes to pain, theorizing grinds to a halt. Just as error is the way PPRs get to the real, Siebers gets to the real with pain. It also helps distinguish disability studies from body studies. As Siebers writes, "There are only a few images of pain acceptable to current body theory, and none of them is realistic from the standpoint of people who suffer pain daily." So Siebers advocates "restoring a sense of the realism of the disability body" to body theory.[11]

Although he says pain is real, he also cautions us to resist the "temptation to view disability and pain as more real than their opposites. . . . The disabled body is not more real than the able body—and no less real."[12] Perhaps it is that moment that illustrates both the strengths and the problems of such an approach. Given what Siebers has written, it is difficult to formulate exactly his position. To confuse the point further, Siebers says in the same paragraph that "current theories of reality . . . prefer complexity to simplicity. . . . They lop off a great deal of reality in the process, most notably, the hard simple realism of the body."[13] In advocating a hard and simple view of the body, he asserts rather than proves.

But how can the body be simple? Or another way of asking this is: how simple can the body be? Even pain, which seems like a primal, unmediated force, is, as David Morris and Ronald Schleifer have shown us, a very complex phenomenon and by no means simple in our understanding it or even feeling it.[14]

For Siebers, the problem with ideological or ethical views of the body is that they are prescriptive. So current theories "are part of a rhetoric that exists less to explain how the body works than to make claims about how it 'ought' to work in the society we all apparently desire."[15] How strange then that Siebers switches from the issue of the reality of the body by saying that "the most urgent issue for disability studies is the political struggle of people with disabilities, and this struggle requires a realistic conception of the disabled body."[16] This is a change of register from the theoretical to realpolitik. But when he has just cautioned us against theories that derive from "ought," he uses the word "requires." There is not a lot of linguistic space, in my lexicon, between "ought" and "requires."

To take this a step further, Siebers moves to an even more prescriptive statement: "The number-one objective for disability studies, then, is to make disability an object of general knowledge and thereby to awaken political consciousness to the distasteful prejudice called 'ableism.'"[17] While Siebers and I both believe this to be true, we don't entirely agree on what that general knowledge might be. For Siebers it is self-evident that "we all seem to share a basic intuition about what it means to be human."[18] Linked to that, we should then all share a basic intuition about what it means to be a disabled human or being. But it is precisely the point that we as beings don't share either, Siebers's claim to humanism notwithstanding. If we did all share the same intuition, then how could we say that the basic project of disability studies is some kind of general knowledge? Are we all supposed to have that knowledge in our intuition? And isn't one of the main points of postmodernism that we can see how identities are falsely constructed and deconstruct them in the hopes of showing how that "basic intuition" isn't inherent but learned, and often wrongly learned in the form of prejudice and self-interest?

Although Siebers cautions us that theories seem somehow in opposition to the real of the body, he then states, "identities are complex theories about the social and moral world."[19] This is an interesting point in that it changes the very notion of theory, if theory can be incorporated into one's own identity. Perhaps we need a longer quotation from Siebers to help his assertion make sense:

> Realism entails a recognition of the significant causal factors of the
> social world by which the identities of groups and individuals are

created. Identities are not infinitely interpretable, then, because they obey the rules of their formation and have strong connections to other cultural representations. Their verification and analysis rely on a coordination with the real world and a coordination between interconnected hypotheses about and experiences with society, which means that identity is both pragmatic and epistemic. In short, cultural identities, because they respond to natural and cultural factors, make certain actions possible and present a resource for understanding society and its many meanings.[20]

Siebers is saying that identities aren't infinitely malleable because they are connected to other cultural representations and coordinate with the "real world." Identities are based on "interconnected hypotheses and experiences" and so are both pragmatic and point toward systems of meanings. The problem here comes from the reliance of identities on other signs and meanings in society. So can something that is real, from the point of view of the person with the identity, rely for its quality of being real on something like "cultural representations"? This would mean, for example, that my being Jewish would be reliant on images of Jews on television and in film. Yes, to some extent that is true, but that just moves the question of what is real into the realm of filmic representation. And a move like that puts the real into a kind of deep existential doubt. Likewise, if identities are theories about the world, then you could of course say that a theory is real when it enters the realm of action, as in, the theory of the social model is real as it interacts with policy decisions and political acts. But because it is a "theory" it is also disprovable and therefore can't be an absolute sign of the real.

I'm using Siebers to illustrate the complexity of trying to come up with a "real" that trumps theory. Although he is not an adherent of PPR, Siebers's analysis nevertheless shares some contours with PPR. Each of the claims of both appears to be true, but when assembled into a model, these claims seem so reliant on other claims—so complex is one way of putting it or so hedged might be another way—that the full force of the argument is dissolved in its nuances. Instead of kicking the rock, PPRs would take photos of it, analyze it, and put it in a geological museum to show how it is both real and also subject to complex analysis.

One of the best critiques of dismodernism comes from Robert McRuer, who argues with one point I made—that disability could be the identity that underlies all the other identities. McRuer notes correctly that having one common denominator for all identities would itself just replace one current, regnant paradigm for others that had lost some currency. He advocates, rather than one identity "trumping," as he says, all the others, that there be coalition and mutual investigation and political action. That is a good point and one that I would not wish to refute. I don't quite think I meant that disability should trump other identities, but rather I at least wanted to say that the mechanisms of exclusion and attitudes and practices toward the body were perhaps paradigmatic of other forms of exclusion and subjection.

McRuer also makes the statement, again I think correct, that my view that there was a simple view of identity was disproved by the work of Eve Sedgewick, Lisa Duggins, and others who always saw the complexity of identity. As McRuer says in the title and the body of his essay, "we were never identified," echoing Bruno Latour's phrase "we were never human." Again, the point is well taken, but there is a distinction to be made between complex academic analyses and general perceptions. If McRuer had discussed this issue with an African American during the civil rights movement and claimed that his or her identity as an African American was an amorphous, shifting thing, McRuer might have found some pushback. Likewise with each emerging identity group. It may well be that groups have debates within their borders about tactics, definitions, and so on, but in the midst of political struggle, there is less doubt about identity. This is also the case with the majority of citizens, who view, rather unproblematically, the identity of their fellow citizens or "illegal immigrants." It is true that identity is positional and temporal—if you are within a group, you may see things one way, while outsiders may see things another way; first wave might differ from second wave. So when I spoke of identity as a "dead end," I was speaking of a particular moment with particular stakeholders. And I would still stand by my point that within disability studies and activism there had been at that time, and perhaps is even now, a strong impetus to see disability as a discrete and strongly delineated entity.

One of the most careful and sustained critiques of dismodernism is made by Anna Mollow. [21] She gives a very close reading of many of the points I make, and while I can't go into each one here, one of her two basic assertions is that I seem to critique poststructuralism and postmodernism, which she believed in 2004 had much to offer to disability studies. Her other major critique is that I seem to oppose the erotic and disability. To the first point I would say that Mollow does a nice job of pointing out when I contradict myself in a number of different works and within the same work. Nevertheless, the point I think I was making is that I am in fact someone whose theory depends on a number of postmodern insights— most particularly Foucault's insights—and yet I find fault with the way many postmodernists view disability or rather don't view disability at all. I probably should have said in the dismodernism essay, as I have in other works, that theorists like Derrida, Lacan, Butler, Deleuze, and others have some very important things to say about fragmented, incomplete bodies, deafness, and the like.

As for the critique that I make an opposition between the erotic and disability, I think and hope what I was saying is that others make that opposition. I would never, and should not ever, say that disability is not erotic. In saying, for example, that the Venus di Milo was considered one of the most beautiful and erotic sculptures in the Western world and an actual woman who looked like her was not, I took the liberty of not including myself in the conglomerate I called the "Western" world. I also did not include the currently very limited group of people who visit disability porn websites and wish to have sex with amputees and the like. Another thing I did not point out was that there is a growing trend to include very attractive disabled people in advertising and the media—usually Deaf people, wheelchair athletes, and single or double amputees with prostheses (like Aimee Mullins, the pre-homicide Oscar Pistorius, or Heather Mills), who are increasingly seen as erotic ideals.

Perhaps as part of a similar reaction to social constructionism, feminist materialists are returning to a qualified sense of "the body." Sarah Ahmed and others have written about emotions, while the turn to neuroscience has reintroduced the materiality of the body, according to Victoria Pitts-Taylor and a growing group of aestheticians, as well as philosophers and literary critics. Materialist feminists like Stacy Alaimo and Susan Hekman link up ecological concerns with animal rights as well as disability studies to create a matrix of questions about the material side of existence. Jasbir Puar and Mel Chen continue in that vein by exploring queerness, postcoloniality, and disability studies. All of these scholars and others seek to find points of connection among identities and thus change our conception of identities in ways that I would call dismodern.

Indeed, work that centers on the human-animal divide or nexus becomes very important in the discussion of disability. In these discussions, the human subject has been decentered in the realm of animal rights and studies. One reviewer of *Bending Over Backwards* chose to review the book along with Cary Wolfe's *Animal Rites*. Celeste Langan saw those two books as related in a key way, noting that each of us was considering an outcast group (animals and people with disabilities) and trying to revise the fiction of the human by making those outcast groups central to any discussion of identity. Wolfe advocates a posthuman viewpoint, whereas I offer a "dismodernist" one. Langan notes that I wish to move disability studies "beyond a (liberal) politics of inclusion." Wolfe too wants to move beyond simple notions of including or excluding animals in the discussion of rights and representation.

The animal-human connection has had a great deal of influence in academic and other discussions, but particularly in the work of Peter Singer, who is the foremost theoretician and philosopher of animal rights. In his work the animal and the human seem to converge with a violent impact. Singer argues that animals, because they can make decisions and feel pain and suffering, should be treated with care and respect. Eating them is not indicative of such care. More recently, Singer and others have suggested that what we call human rights should be extended to primates. All well and good for those who support animal rights, but Singer takes the further, for him logical, step of saying that if there isn't a bright, clear line between the animal and the human, we should define these kinds of life by their capacities—the ability to make decisions, avoid pain, and seek pleasure. If we do that, then certain kinds of humans don't fit into those criteria, and they, by their existence, impinge on the ability of other humans to live and enjoy their lives. These borderline cases are people in comas, severely brain-damaged people, and the like. That is, humans who can't make decisions, avoid pain, and seek pleasure should not have the rights of animals and humans who can. Moreover, since the care for such borderline humans is so expensive and time-consuming, the cost deprives others of resources and conditions to make their lives livable. [22]

We could say that Singer's position—proanimal, antiseverely disabled—highlights some of the problems I have raised as issues in a dismodernist era. The normal standard of the human as abstractly the category of the "normal" has been displaced or opened up (depending on your view). The hegemonic notion that if one is human, one must be the neoclassical measure of all things gives way to a Nietzschean vision of the human as one type of phenomenon among many. If we argue, as we do in disability studies, that people with disabilities should have the rights that all humans do, should we stop there and resist the argument that animals should have such rights? If we eschew the idea of human-centered "normality," are we not obligated to cross the human-animal divide? So would that mean that a disability-activist point of view would inherently be vegan as well? Sunaura Taylor's work on veganism and disability argues for that position. [23] Siebers's notion that we all have an inherent sense of what it means to be human seems contradicted in this new point of view, in which we would have to include our primate siblings and perhaps our dolphin cousins in the human family or our family in theirs. Not so simple that inherent sense of what it means to be human.

The work of Georgio Agamben takes us around this block in a somewhat different way. I hadn't read Agamben when I talked about dismodernism, but it seems his work is directly relevant.[24] Agamben poses the concept of "bare life" or "homo sacer" to name that borderline state that Singer discusses as well. There are categories of the human that are considered more *zoe*, that is, purely animal, than *bios*, life as inserted into and defined by the state. These bare forms of life outside of the life of the state might be called "abject," according to Julia Kristeva.[25] For Agamben, the state is in fact founded on the primary and early exclusion of bare life, and the resulting modern versions of this are the death camps and the harvesting of organs from comatose patients. We could link up Singer and Agamben by saying that the primary exclusion that creates the state is bare life that also could be defined as barely human. In Singer's case, the barely human includes the severely disabled. So to give this an Agambian twist, the state historically has been founded on the exclusion of the severely disabled. Or another way of putting this is that the severely disabled made the state possible by affording the exclusion that defines inclusion, as I proposed in chapter 1.

If I had read Agamben ten years ago, I might have said that dismodernism advocates the defining of the posthuman by the inclusion of the abject, bare life, the disabled—in other words, including the imperfect, the interdependent, the nonideal in the very sphere of the polis, the agora, and so on. To say so might in fact be a contradictory idea since it seems that exclusion is the very basis for group formation. So wouldn't the inclusion of the abject or *zoe* in fact dissolve the social and political structure? In a way it might, which is why it seems that getting disability to be recognized as an identity like other identity groups has been so difficult. And we have heard the response that because disability is such a large and varied identity, it threatens other more established identity groups.

One final point: I've been told that students always seize on my comment that disabled parking should not be a subset of normal parking, but the other way around. I recognize that this proposal is not simply utopian but impractical as well. But I offered it up as a challenge to conventional ways of thinking. If we believe that interdependence and need are central components of existing in a dismodernist modality, then why should the need to park more closely to a store be assigned only to people with disabilities? The fact that only 5 percent of people with disabilities use wheel-chairs, that ambulatory immobility is not the salient feature of disability, should lead us to understand that parking near the entrance of a store is something that many people will need to do. It would be more interesting to set up a large row of spaces at a shopping mall and have a sign that says, "If you are having trouble walking longer distances, please park here." I'm sure that sign would self-regulate better than the current model and would cause less animus on the part of people who resent having to park farther away and against those people who park in "handicapped parking" when they "shouldn't."

In the end, dismodernism may be a provocation to thinking differently, but it is not a premature or dangerous idea. It offers a critique of both disability studies and some other identity theories. While allowing for the existence of disability as an identity category, it asks for a raising of the bar when it comes to thinking about identity. If God is the one who says, "I am that I am," then perhaps that definition is too grandiose for mere mortal identities within our current politics. Likewise, the inverse claim "I am not what I am not" is equally reductionist. In the space between sameness and difference, there is a great buffer of uncertainty. To claim that disability identity is finally simple because it is grounded by pain is no more satisfying than claiming that it is grounded by agreed-upon common knowledge. But saying that uncertainty is part of understanding disability identity is not in any way a denial of the validity of being disabled. In fact, according to the tenets of dismodernism, it is an affirmation.

CHAPTER THREE

Disability in the Media

or, Why Don't Disabled Actors Play Disabled Roles?

Perhaps every theory has to contradict itself. If I've been saying that dismodernism allows for a flexible and malleable sense of identity in relationship to disability, then when I think about the notion of actors playing disabled characters, it would seem I would be open to any kind of actor playing any kind of part. Isn't identity what you make of it, rather than an absolute and essential category? You would think so, but in this essay I'm going to be arguing that only disabled actors should play disabled roles.

It's not like we don't see a lot of people with disabilities in film. In some sense, disability is one of the subspecialties of the visual media. From Lon Chaney Jr. playing the Hunchback of Notre Dame to Daniel Day Lewis's portrayal of Christy Brown in *My Left Foot* to Sam Worthington playing Jake Sully in *Avatar*, from the wheelchair-using dancer on *Glee* to the son with cerebral palsy on *Breaking Bad*, media loves disability. People with disabilities are portrayed in the media as present, in the sense of ubiquitous, always marked as different and yet rarely if ever played by actors with disabilities. Why is that?

Cinema and television use popular and knowable narratives and then tweak them a bit here and there. Disabilities are part of that narrative. Physical disabilities appear in the popular imagination in a variety of ways, notably as challenges or tragedies, and affective while cognitive disorders have a somewhat different role. Intellectual disabilities, most particularly in the case of people with Down syndrome, and autism tend to function in the media as states of existence designed to evoke the compassion of the viewer. Most commonly, audiences are called upon to produce a limited range of responses from sympathy or pity to some kind of beneficent granting of limited personhood to such characters. The more lovable and understandable the characters become, the more likely the film or television show will succeed. And the ultimate point about the function of such narratives is that they end up making the audience feel good about itself and its own "normality."

Affective and anxiety disorders seem to provoke a different audience involvement than do intellectual and cognitive disabilities. If the affective disorder falls into the realm of anxiety, depression, delusion, or schizophrenia, the film or television special (never a series) will revolve around that character "going mad." The madness, in turn, will then symbolize the response we might all have to a dehumanizing, stressful, disabling, and demeaning society. The character becomes a tragic stand-in for any viewer facing the human condition. Some movies, like *A Beautiful Mind*, *The Soloist*, and *The Fisher King*, follow the descent of the character into madness while trying to offer some kind of cure, control, or redemption at the end. *Silver Linings Playbook* offers us, well, silver linings about affective disorders.

Obsessive-compulsive disorder seems to straddle the divide between tragedy and redemption, as well as between tragedy and comedy. The standard representation of OCD in film and other narrative forms is to see the obsessive behavior as a combination of amusing and debilitating. One scenario turns the person with OCD into a kind of lovable nut, or what I like to call a disability "mascot." The mascotization of disabilities produces warm, cuddly, lovable representations. The television show *Monk* mainly does this, while also showing how disability can itself be ability. Monk is a detective whose Holmes-like skills are aided by his obsessive behavior. Monk can notice things that others can't and like Sherlock Holmes has a kind of autistic intensity that aids his detective work but hinders his life. Monk "suffers" from his disability and can't function without a personal assistant who hands him sanitizing wipes and coaxes him through his fears. Yet in this case, cure is not an option. In one episode, for example, he decides to go on meds, and although he is personally happier as his symptoms diminish, he becomes a terrible detective. So he eventually renounces the meds, goes back to his tortured but amusing self, and returns to super-sleuthing. Shows like *The Big Bang Theory* group conditions like Asperger's syndrome with OCD in loveable and amusing characters like Sheldon.

Reality TV shows have even gotten into the affective disorder act. *Obsessed* is a series that follows people with OCD and other compulsions.

These include people who are agoraphobic, those who pick their faces, pull their hair out, count compulsively, hoard, and so on. The series does not turn people with OCD into mascots, but rather portrays them as symptoms in need of cure. Any individual episode is painful to watch, but the people themselves become objects of interest, compassion, fear, and pity. The aim of the show is to let us know that cures are readily available for scary diseases.

In *Obsession: A History* I raised the point about how we categorize being obsessed. In one sense, we live in a culture that values obsession. We think that the best and brightest should be obsessed with their work, their lives, their sex lives, and so on. At the same time, we subcategorize a section of such behavior as "too much." Those who are too obsessed fall into a clinical category. The social, political, and ideological surround creates a state of desire for obsession and fear of obsession. The key way to tell if you are too obsessed is to note whether you feel pain or suffering in regard to your obsessions and compulsions. If you do, then you are clinically obsessed.

This concept that the ability to choose is the difference between good and bad obsession is a crucial point. If you choose to be obsessed in work, athletics, or sex, that is a good thing. If you cannot help but count the number of times you brush your teeth or the number of steps you need to cross a threshold, and you can't stop, then you are pathological. Your ability to choose is the key difference between pathology and passion. Linked to this is how you feel about it. If you do such things, are happy about them, then you will not choose to stop. If you do such things, want to stop, or are told by family members, friends, or lovers that you should stop, and you can't, then you are pathological or, putting it another way, disabled.

It shouldn't take too much effort, as I pointed out earlier, to see that the element of choice and the element of "how you feel about it" are key signposts along the way of neoliberal, consumer society, which is based on the idea of the consumer who has the power to choose to buy products and who is happy to do so. So with OCD personal suffering comes from wanting to but being unable to. And suffering comes from being in an environment that pinpoints the kinds of things you are doing as unproductive and worthy of stopping. An article in the *New York Times*, for example, showcases a man who obsessively builds large gardens with mosaics made from small pebbles. Jeffrey Bale is described as picking through four hundred pounds of pebbles "and [finding] only two dozen stones that would work for this project, an ornate pathway and sunken garden mosaic" in the garden of Tony Shalhoub—ironically, or perhaps not, the actor who plays

Monk. The article makes the obvious connection between such painstaking activity and OCD, and Mr. Bale responds, "It's not a disorder if you channel it into something productive."[1]

OCD as it is understood by the general public is a discrete disease. It has developed over time into something incontrovertible, and recent work seeks to locate its origin in brain chemistry, structure, or genetics. It feels palpable and real, and the suffering it produces is real as well. In that sense, OCD is primed to be sucked into the media mill. It has dramatic possibilities as ordinary people seem to be fingered for torment by mysterious and diabolic forces. However, my own work suggests that the causes are not mysterious. In fact, I argue that there is a deep cultural involvement in the genesis and production of this illness. And the media, for one, is implicated both for publicizing it as the disease of the month, for narrativizing it in familiar ways, and for dramatizing the dilemma of the person with the disorder. I'm not blaming the media here, just pointing out how a disease can be proliferated through the dispersal of images and stories about it. In the case of OCD, for example, the disorder has gone from an extremely rare disease in the 1950s to one of the four most common disorders in our time. In a mere fifty years or so, OCD has gone from something "had" by one out of one thousand to one in ten. People now routinely say, "I'm so OCD."

The point I want to make is that OCD is a clinical entity, which can mean many things, but one thing it means is that it is part of a social, cultural, medical—that is to say biocultural—milieu. As such it is produced by conscious and unconscious cooperation among medical establishments, individuals, social networks, and families, and their intersection with governmental, media, and corporate entities. This is a complex process that is both essentialist on some level and performative on another. OCD then becomes both a disorder and by extension an identity or a set of identities. How do people who "have" OCD know that they have it? How do they enact their symptoms? How do family members and friends help them to "identify" it?

In this sense the media is more active than simply holding up the proverbial mirror to life. The media is deeply involved in the proliferation of images that help people in the general population diagnose themselves. And the direct-to-consumer advertising for psychoactive drugs such as antidepressants, antipsychotics, and sleeping pills is an intimate part of the matrix that is television viewing. In a sense, the media isn't simply about the portrayal of disabilities, but the de facto advocate of contemporary treatments for affective disorders as well.

Linked to this hegemonic activity is the development of identities to correspond with this (literally) drug-induced citizenship in which one becomes an insurance card-carrying member with "depression" or OCD along with other disorders you have seen on television and in film. That is, one's identity iterated and reiterated on television and in film as a trope and a dramatic plot element—particularly in the form of a knowable, understandable, and delimited character—becomes a familiar feature of everyday life. In turn, television and film narratives often center on how people choose to live with these disease entities, now seen as freestanding and independent of any social or economic forces. For example, there are cinematic possibilities in portraying someone with OCD or depression, but no possibilities of showing in film how OCD develops over time in complex ways and also no possibility of dramatizing the life of someone who is depressed not by a putative biochemical imbalance but because he or she is poor, part of the 99 percent, and so on. In the media, poverty, like disability, is something to be overcome. Both are rarely if ever portrayed as systematic problems; rather, they are routinely seen as individual ones. And we never have a TV series about poverty, only about the side effects of poverty—drugs, prostitution, crime, just as we never have seen a TV series about disability, only about how a disabled character, often minor, makes other "normal" people feel good about themselves.

At this point, I want to explore a contradiction between what I have been saying in this essay and what I've said earlier in this book and elsewhere. That is, I've spent a fair amount of time in my work and writing deconstructing the idea of a monolithic disability identity. I've claimed that what characterizes disability is that it is a shifting, changing, morphing notion of identity that distinguishes itself from other identity categories that seem to have developed, over time, a certain rigidity in definition.

So the example I've often used is that you can become disabled overnight by a car accident or a fall from a horse, while if you are a woman or a person of color, you can't wake up the next day and find yourself a man or a white person. I've said all of this with a lot of qualifications about the shiftiness of all identity categories, but with the assertion that disability identity can lead us to rethinking all identity categories, and as I discussed in the previous chapter, I have coined the term *dismodernism* to point out the way that disability as a category can help us find a postmodern perspective on the aging, antique, and antiquated categories of race, gender, and so on.

Yet recently I've been blogging about the necessity for Hollywood and other large media conglomerates to rethink their attitudes toward having nondisabled actors play disabled characters.[2] Isn't it a contradiction for me to claim that there is no essential identity to disability and then insist on disabled actors playing the role of disabled characters? If I am using critics like Judith Butler to claim that there is something nonessentialist and performative about disability and normality, then why shouldn't nondisabled actors perform the roles of disabled people? And if I maintain the necessity of disabled actors playing disabled roles, am I being rather crudely essentialist?

You could argue that since disability, according to the social model, is in the environment, not in the person, then creating an accommodating environment in which all can perform any theatrical or cinematic role regardless of physical status would be an appropriate action. So if I say that only disabled actors can play disabled parts, aren't I in effect saying that only some people should be accommodated?

Before I come to grips with this problem, I think it will be necessary to present the lay of the land as concerns disability and acting. For a nondisabled actor to take on the role of a disabled person, there are huge incentives. If you want to try for an Academy Award, you would do well to portray a person with a disability. Notable movies of this kind fill the silver screen, from Patty Duke's Helen Keller to Dustin Hoffman's Rainman, from Daniel Day Lewis's portrayal of Christie Brown to Tom Cruise as Ron Kovic in *Born on the Fourth of July*, and John Hawkes in *The Sessions*. Yet, in all these cases, the people who starred in these films were nondisabled actors playing disabled roles. So the take-home message here is that films that focus on disability in a central way continue to be made and remain star vehicles for high-profile nondisabled actors.

You would think then, given the appeal of these roles, that characters with disabilities should be rife in the media. Only they are not. Although disability can provide acting opportunities, on television, at least, they are scarce; the *Hollywood Reporter*'s survey for the 2011 season noted that out of a total of six hundred repeating characters on US primetime television shows, only six were characters written to have a disability. And of those, only one was actually played by a disabled actor.[3] Most of the supporting roles in movies will be played by nondisabled people. And the default status for the stereotypical roles—the best friend of the main character, the mother, father, siblings, and so on—will all be conceived of as normal and not disabled.

Why that is has something to do with the economy of visual storytelling in an ableist culture. This in turn comes out of the legacy of eugenics and the current hegemony of ableism itself. If you want to make a film that is about disability in such a culture, then every part of the story has to do with disability. The film has to be, in some sense, obsessed with disability. But if the roving eye of the camera takes its focus off of disability, then disability has to disappear, or it will create a buzz of interference in the storytelling. Instead of disability, to illustrate this point, think of pregnancy. It is quite normal to see a pregnant woman on the street, but if you make one of the characters in a television show pregnant, then you have to provide a whole rationale and back story for the pregnancy. That's why generic mothers in cinematic narratives about children are never pregnant, unless the pregnancy figures into the plot, whereas in real life mothers might be pregnant or not, depending on a host of completely random factors. The same might be said of acne, sore throats, and other bodily ills. Likewise with disability—if the mother of a child in a movie has a disability, and the film isn't about the disability, then the audience will be distracted from the narrative arc by the disability. They will wonder why the "normalcy" of the film is being tampered with. In an ableist culture disability can't just *be*—it has to *mean* something. It has to signify.

In this sense, disability is allegorical—it has to stand for something else—weakness, insecurity, bitterness, frailty, evil, innocence, and so on—and be the occasion for the conveyance of some moral truth—that people are good, can overcome, that we shouldn't discriminate or despair. But, to paraphrase Freud, sometimes an amputated leg is just an amputated leg. That obvious statement can never be true in the world of media narrative, and so an amputated leg is never just that. It must be a character trait, a metaphor, and fit into a plot point, or be a "reveal" to some other character who hasn't seen it, or to the main character who discovers new things about himself or herself in the process of triumphing over the disability. Yet possessing a functional leg is never allegorical, needs no interpretation, and is basically a degree-zero signifier without a referent.

When an actor takes on a role as a person with a disability, he or she is entering a world of signs and meanings that encapsulate the larger society's attitude toward disability. This system of signs and meanings participates in and encourages the nondisabled person's fantasy about disability. Just as Edward Said points out in *Orientalism* that the East was made into the projected fantasy of the West, so have film and television, and the ableist media, projected its image of disability. You learn much more, according to Said, about the West by studying orientalist works that you learn about the East. And with ableist narratives you learn much more about the mindset of a "normal" than you do about the real experience of being a person with a disability. So it might well be that only a nondisabled actor could in fact portray that distorted and biased disability that lives and breathes in ableist culture and that translates so easily to the standard Hollywood film or television series. Just as only someone like Rudolph Valentino could portray the orientalist sheik in the silent movies—being the eroticized but very Western heartthrob who could convey the mytheme of the sexuality of the orient. In the same way, the nondisabled actor can eroticize and embody the stereotypes and clichés inherent in the regnant ideology around disability.

A nondisabled actor has literally to transform him- or herself in order to portray a disabled person. Audiences and critics enjoy that transformative ability, and it is surely tied up with our basic ideas of theatricality. We are used to the idea that an actor transforms him- or herself by means of makeup, mental preparation, and now even computer-graphical assist. In fact there is something mercurial and protean about being an actor. We admire the hours of cosmetic and prosthetic work that goes into transforming the likes of Brad Pitt into the likes of the aged Benjamin Button.

But we are now less willing to approve, and this is where the complexity comes in, when we transform actors from a dominant identity group to one that is not. So, for example, the practice of using blackface was widely appreciated and prized by white audiences of theater and film until attitudes toward people of color became much changed, beginning in the 1930s. Despite performances by Al Jolson in the 1929 classic *The Jazz Singer*, Fred Astaire in *Top Hat*, and, as late as 1938 to 1941, Judy Garland repeatedly, in *Everyone Sing* (1938), *Babes in Arms* (1939), and *Babes on Broadway* (1941), the latter two directed by Busby Berkeley, the practice faded out entirely from dramatic works by the 1950s and 1960s. Blackface may have taken a very late bow, but having white actors portray Native Americans, Asians, Indians, Arabs, and others continued well into the latter half of the twentieth century, until consciousness-raising and awareness of racism ended that practice only as recently as twenty-five years ago.

It is now almost universally acknowledged that when it comes to most racial groups, actors from within the tradition of those groups are preferred to actors from outside. No one doubts, for example, that Ben Kingsley can do a pretty good job of playing Gandhi, but in 1982 such a practice was tolerated, whereas now it might not be. It is currently acceptable for Morgan Freeman to play Nelson Mandela in Clint Eastwood's *Invictus*, although South African actors decried the limited roles for them in this film. Freeman as an African American is seen as having enough kinship with black Africans to make the transition by Hollywood, at least by US if not by South African standards. The Creative Workers Union in South Africa protested, saying, "we want more South African actors because we do have some great talent to take on these strong roles in these stories." South African actor Florence Mesebe analyzed the situation thus: "South African actors are never going to be good enough, because we don't have the Hollywood tag. We are tired of the Hollywood box office excuse."[4]

These arguments concerning ethnicity and national origin seem to ring less forcefully to the public because those in the English-speaking world routinely see US, UK, Australian, and New Zealand actors playing each other's nationality, as well as playing Russians, Eastern Europeans, Greeks, Italians, Jews, and the like.[5] Within the larger category of those who are currently considered "whites," there is less trouble with interchangeability.

So how do we parse these predilections and taboos? Again, I'd return to the issue of choice. Nationalities and even ethnicities, particularly where there are no overly stereotyped physical features, are not seen as rooted in the concept of normality, but rather in the concept of diversity. One can choose to move from South Africa to the UK, and if one is white, there is little discrimination to be faced, particularly in the assimilated generations. Actors, therefore, are well within their rights to play these kind of parallel roles, and their skill in adopting accents, as actors like Meryl Streep or Jude Law do routinely, is part of their mimetic profession. Thus nationality does not seem inappropriate for actors to take on in their roles, although race does. Disability has been seen as fair game for actors, but in a sense it is ontologically more like race in the sense that it is not a state of being one can choose.

This element of choice is paramount in something like Clint Eastwood's *Million Dollar Baby*, now infamous in disability circles. When it was released, it was roundly criticized for its pessimistic vision of life for a disabled woman. But few criticized Eastwood for not casting a disabled actress in the main role. The reason for that is obvious—Maggie had to go from a physically intact athlete to a quadriplegic in the course of the film. The skill of the actor and the director would involve a transformation that had no element of choice in it (except of course the choice to die). So a central concept in a film like this is that the disabled person is a person without a choice, and therefore the actor who plays the person has to be normal to counter, in some sense, this message of hopelessness (lack of choice) by letting the audience know in a de facto way that the actor, while playing someone who has no choice, himself or herself does have a choice.

That is, although the character is without a choice regarding his or her disability, the audience will always know that the actor has many choices. In fact, to return to the issue of the transformation of the nondisabled actor into a person with a disability, which is often the subject of film publicity, the salient point for the audience is that the actor is not disabled—but that the magic of CGI, makeup, and prosthetics magically and cinematically transforms the actor into the disabled character, as it did with Marion Cotillard in *Rust and Bone*. The audience can rest comfortably assured that the central character may appear to be disabled but isn't really a disabled person, only a nondisabled actor playing a role. The cinematic experience is a form of make-believe whose fantastic nature is revealed when the time comes for Hilary Swank to stride across the stage and accept her Oscar. We know she won't be ambulating using a wheelchair with a sip-straw control. She won't choose to die in obscurity over a disability, but rather will live in Hollywood glory to accept her award.

The star system makes it hard for disabled actors to fit in. Stars tend to be interchangeable parts in a system of production. Their "normality" is a sign of their ability to transform. Transformation and choice, two basic tenets of the neoliberal system based on lifestyle and niche marketing, are touchstones in a system that promotes individuality and self-actualization. Class is never portrayed in film as operating in ultimately disabling ways. One's class in this view is only the place where you start as you transform through choice and hard work. And if you are upper class in film, then your narrative will be about how you suffer from being too rich and have to find yourself through adopting the values and viewpoint of a middle-class or poor person. Each of us, so the story goes, can become anything we want if only we have the will, the drive, and the dedication. The "normal" actor, then, embodies this mythology of class and bodily open-endedness, while the disabled actor is seen as a grim reminder that transformation is not possible, except in limited ways.

If disability represents, in the popular imagination, a tragic fate in which choice is removed, while at the same time it acts as a kind of frightening and disfiguring prospect for audiences who can only too easily imagine themselves transformed into a disabled person by the simple swerve of a car on the highway, a virulent disease, or a malfunction of a gene, then the role of the media historically has been to provide comfort to them. The comfort comes from the triumphant scenario in which the main disabled character overcomes the limitations of the impairment to become the leader of, say, the antiwar movement, or a famous blind-deaf writer, or any other accomplished professional. The comfort also comes from seeing that person accepted with all their limitations by friends, family, lovers, and the general public—which includes the audience, who learns to see that person as "human." Indeed, the greatest comfort comes from knowing that the character is being play-acted by a normal person. The fear of fragmentation and destruction of ego is compensated for by the notion that "it's only a movie."

Some of these points are illustrated in the film *Avatar*. Jake Sully, played by Sam Worthington, a nondisabled actor, is a paraplegic who lost the use of his legs in war as a marine. At one point in the film, we see his atrophied legs as he wheels his chair frontally toward the camera. This shot is in some sense the "money shot" that verifies to the audience that the physical body of the actor is indeed that of a paraplegic—while of course in reality it is not. As in *Rust and Bone*, a kind of sexual truism is allowed, as we see naked Stephanie having sex, her two stumped legs up in the air—comfortable in knowing these impairments are a product of CGI. Part of the visual frisson of seeing those atrophied legs is knowing that this is one among many other special effects that have no contractual bearing on the reality of the actor's actual body. In fact, *Avatar* is about nothing if not transformation, since Jake becomes a larger-than-life blue avatar through the miracle of DNA, biotechnology, and of course CGI and 3D. In fact, the realism of the 3D effect guarantees the realism of the live-action part of the film, which also "guarantees" the character's disability. That disability disappears in the movie whenever Jake enters his avatar, and, given the film's logic, the unreal world of the avatar eventually becomes more real than the live-action part of the film. In this paradisiacal world of the primeval forest of Pandora, Jake is one with nature, able to perform acts of physical prowess and agilely use his superhuman mobility. So the bargain with the audience is that you get to have a disabled character, who remains disabled at the end of the film, even turning down the villain's offer to give him back his legs through expensive medical cures, but that indeed that character can still transform to become a nondisabled character. And of course, in reality, Sam Worthington had the ability to walk into the Academy Awards on his own two feet. Everyone will be assured that the movie is after all only a movie. And disability is after all only a trope, a signifying event, an allegorical state of being.

To return to my main argument and contradiction, I think it fair and right that disabled actors should play disabled roles, or as a UK organization says, "Pay Us! Don't Play Us." The general public, however, based on responses to the blogs I've written, are torn about this proposition, and many feel that delimiting what an actor can and can't do is an abrogation of freedom of speech and a denial of what it is that actors do. And then I myself have argued for the fluidity of the identity category of disability, so why would I then argue that we should limit roles to actors who are "actually" disabled in the particular way that the character is?

My response would be that in the best of possible worlds, all actors should play all parts. As my colleague Rosemarie Garland-Thomson questioned recently: why shouldn't disabled actors be cast in nondisabled roles?[6] But the current state of affairs perpetuates ableism by reinforcing the audiences' expectations both that disability is a state to be magically transformed and that nondisabled actors are the high priests who reenact this sacrament every time they don a disability for a role and then remove it when they go home at night. This state of affairs also ghettoizes stardom so that only nondisabled characters can become stars, which in turn emphasizes that disability is an abnormal state that needs to be patrolled and marginalized by casting directors and unreceptive audiences.

Indeed, if we only consider issues of fairness, it would make sense that a discriminated-against group of actors—those with disabilities—are in need of work. I am not suggesting a quota system or affirmative action, but some of the principles of those systems might well be applied to the casting of actors. Right now, it makes little sense for a young person with disabilities to imagine a career in acting. I recently asked Matt Fraser, one of the more successful disabled actors, whether things were improving for disabled actors, and he told me that he didn't think they were. In what other profession would it be acceptable to discriminate against an identity and get away with it? In what other profession would we counsel young people to forget their hopes and dreams because of rampant prejudice against the kind of person they are? The state of affairs is not acceptable, and only when we routinely see disabled actors playing disabled and nondisabled roles will the stereotypes perpetuated in the media be eliminated. While it may seem like a rarified complaint to lodge against Hollywood, it is actually crucial to the goals of disability awareness and disability studies.

CHAPTER FOUR

Depression and Disability

Another aspect of identity strikes us—the idea that one identity can transform radically into another. Perhaps the most common transformation is for a person to become depressed. We routinely see ourselves and our friends take a turn from "normal" to depressed. And so a logical question to ask is whether depression can be a disability.

I don't think that anyone would doubt that the symptoms of the most severe kinds of depression are disabilities. If you can't get out of bed for a very long period of time, can't function, have lost all connection to life, and wish to die or kill yourself, and this lasts for a very long time, then this state of being is clearly both an impairment and a disabling state of being, at that.

But I want to discuss not that limited experience and definition, but the kind of depression that many people have and for which they are treated. I am talking about the depression that is listed in the *Diagnostic and Statistical Manual* (*DSM*), the bible of psychological and psychiatric diagnosis, as a "major depressive episode" or "major depressive disorder." According to the *DSM*'s fourth edition, in order for a person to be diagnosed with this disorder, he or she needs to have five of the following symptoms, and those symptoms need to have lasted for a minimum of two weeks:

(1) depressed mood most of the day, nearly every day, as indicated by either subjective report (e.g., feels sad or empty) or observation made by others (e.g., appears tearful). **Note:** In children and adolescents, can be irritable mood.

(2) markedly diminished interest or pleasure in all, or almost all,

activities most of the day, nearly every day (as indicated by either subjective account or observation made by others)

(3) significant weight loss when not dieting or weight gain (e.g., a change of more than 5% of body weight in a month), or decrease or increase in appetite nearly every day. **Note:** In children, consider failure to make expected weight gains.

(4) insomnia or hypersomnia nearly every day

(5) psychomotor agitation or retardation nearly every day (observable by others, not merely subjective feelings of restlessness or being slowed down)

(6) fatigue or loss of energy nearly every day

(7) feelings of worthlessness or excessive or inappropriate guilt (which may be delusional) nearly every day (not merely self-reproach or guilt about being sick)

(8) diminished ability to think or concentrate, or indecisiveness, nearly every day (either by subjective account or as observed by others)

(9) recurrent thoughts of death (not just fear of dying), recurrent suicidal ideation without a specific plan, or a suicide attempt or a specific plan for committing suicide.[1]

It is probably true that many of us have experienced five or more such symptoms for two weeks. And indeed, depending on which statistics you buy, about 16 percent of people have been depressed in the course of a lifetime, and in any given year, 6 to 7 percent of Americans are depressed, about the same number as those who are diabetic.[2] Given that number, if such people were considered disabled, then a much greater percentage of the population would be disabled than the current generally used number of 15 percent.

I don't believe that we should consider people with mild-to-moderate depression disabled, and it will be the burden of the rest of this essay to prove my point. In order to do so, I will have to analyze the nature of this form of psychic distress and consider whether it is an impairment or not. To do that, I'll have to discuss whether depression is a disease (that can be cured) and touch on the general issue of mental "illness." And to do that, I'll have to examine the disease model and the serotonin hypothesis insofar as it relates to depression. I'll have to go into this level of detail because the disease model of depression in current medicine is loosely based on the assumption that depression is a chemical imbalance in need of correction through the use of drugs known as selective serotonin uptake inhibitors (SSRIs) or a neurological condition in need of the same remedy. In current psychiatric parlance, depression is a biological disease located in the brain, and we know that, so the argument goes, because when we give people drugs that raise their serotonin levels, they get better. So lowered serotonin levels create the biological brain disease called depression. I can guarantee that this essay will end up discussing the issues of impairment and disability, but before getting there I will have to lay rather extensive groundwork for my argument, which will rely on my providing a biocultural explanation of this complex phenomenon.

Before beginning I want to make a disclaimer. I know there are many people who are deeply unhappy and whose pain is real concerning their unhappiness. I know that many people suffer intense psychic pain and distress, as well as enervating lethargy accompanied by a dulled and muted emotional life, and I am very aware than many people who suffer in this way have taken SSRIs with excellent results. None of that is in question in this essay, nor should it be. These are individual choices made with the advice of one's physician, and I don't think anyone should casually interfere with that collaboration and the options that arise from that collaboration. What I am discussing is how we think about this kind of depression individually and culturally and how we think we can best help ourselves and others who are in pain. But it is not at all obvious to me that we should take the regnant (and temporary—since most models in psychiatry change every thirty years or so) explanatory system and convince ourselves that this time we have finally found the proper way of thinking about psychic distress and how to cure it. I have already had many discussions with my friends who define themselves as depressed and who take SSRIs with considerable relief of their symptoms, and those discussions have been intense and heartfelt. This is not an abstract academic conversation for them, and though many have not done research or read deeply in the field, their own personal experiences, experiments, and narratives include the explanation that theirs is a disease based on a chemical imbalance in the brain called depression, and there is a cure for that disease called SSRIs with interesting names like Prozac, Selexa, Paxil, and Lexapro. To them and others I ask that you allow the possibility that what I am writing could be true and join me and others in trying to find and explore the many truths that make up the complexity of being depressed in our era. In exchange I will try to include your reality and experiences in what I am saying.

What is depression? As I tried to explain in my book *Obsession: A History*, there is a particular problem with psychiatric disorders that makes them unlike other medical disorders. As opposed to many physical diseases, there is no discrete entity we could call depression. Instead, the *DSM* definition of depression is a grab bag of symptoms that could easily also comprise many other diagnostic categories—listlessness, insomnia, drowsiness, low energy, digestive problems, brain fog, inability to concentrate, decreased libido, suicidal impulses, and a checklist of many others. These have been grouped variously under many rubrics throughout history. Indeed, the state of depression we now accept as a category really did not exist before the 1950s. Its rise is chronicled in a number of books.[3] The inclusion or exclusion of symptoms is based on a complex algorithm of politics (both internal to the psychiatric profession and external to it), social custom, ethnic and national mores, and many other factors that come to bear each time the *DSM* is revised.

The issue of politics in the formation of *DSM* categories has been well documented, and I won't repeat the major points here.[4] Suffice it to say that there are intense political and economic interests being brought to bear on the formation and relevance of diagnostic categories. The players include big pharma, government regulatory agencies, advertising, and other powerful interests. But there are also distinct cultural norms to be considered. In the United States, we live in a culture that defines normal life as happy. Our Declaration of Independence offers us the Jeffersonian notion of happiness as something worth pursuing along with life and liberty.[5] No other country in the world was founded on such a premise. Indeed, there are cultures that expect normal life to be painful, difficult, and even tragic. The Greek culture, for one, might be based on a more tragic vision in which their motto could be said to be the downbeat Sophoclean assessment, "count no man happy until he is dead." Thomas Hobbes famously (or infamously) described life as "nasty, brutish, and short." Yet the expectation in the United States is that citizens will live lives, if nothing major comes to trouble us, as happy ones. Sorrow, when it comes, will be seen as an abnormal state. Indeed, normal sorrow doesn't really exist anymore, according to Allan V. Horrowitz and Jerome C. Wakefield. Instead sorrow and sadness have been transformed into something verging on the pathological. In his *The Anti-Depressant Era*,[6] David Healy describes the way physicians in the 1950s and '60s were trained by drug companies to see depression as an underlying problem in many of their patients who had heretofore not been regarded as having a psychological problem. As part of one of the first advertising campaigns for a drug, Merck, the manufacturer of Elavil, printed and sent in 1961 fifty thousand copies of a book called *Recognizing the Depressed Patient*[7] to general practitioners throughout the United States. Frank J. Ayd Jr., who wrote the book for Merck, says early on in the text: "depressions are among the most common illnesses encountered by the general practitioner. . . . Depressive illnesses rank high in the case-load of the family doctor and . . . he treats the majority of these patients himself." Ayd goes on to say, "this monograph has been written solely to assist the non-psychiatrist to recognize depressive illnesses."[8] The idea was that patients who presented to the general physician as tired, anxious, sleepless, and so on were actually manifesting the symptoms of an underlying depression.

In that era, advertising companies began, for the first time, to market psychoactive drugs. For example, to continue the campaign, Merck also made a vinyl record of blues songs with Elavil ads on the inside jacket cover and pharmacological indications inserted in the jacket, providing these free to physicians in a continued effort to connect general depression in culture to psychopharmacological solutions, even if only subliminally suggested by the album. The songs chosen echoed the symptoms of depression: "Blues in My Heart,"[9] "Rocks in My Bed,"[10] "Blues in the Night,"[11] and "How Long, How Long Blues,"[12] among others. The lyrics (indicated in the footnotes) single out insomnia, hopelessness, and suicide as symptoms of depression.

Aside from the substantial push in the latter half of the twentieth century to alloy depression and antidepressants as integrally linked, another general tactic was to see depression as an individual problem. With the breakdown of community and the extended family inherent in the development of the suburbs at midcentury and a vision of existential loneliness as a way of life, depression was seen as an individual's own problem. The biological explanations associated with the chemical-imbalance theory of depression, first put forth in the late 1950s and early 1960s, eliminated the Freudian family web and went for the sole proprietorship of the individual brain. When you are depressed, it is you who suffer and no one else. Depression isn't defined as a communal activity or one that results from a set of environmental circumstances that have become normalized to appear almost undetectable. Depression is never seen as a consequence of the multilayered exigencies of life in the postwar United States.

Beginning in this era and extending to the current moment, only the individual is treated for depression. Yet as complex and social animals, humans rarely feel anything solely on their own. Mirror neurons, according to some neuroscientists, make us apes in the basic sense of aping each other's feelings and even postural attitudes. If we want to be less neurological, we could say that humans are empathetic to those with whom they have a sense of connection. Sadness can get passed around as easily as laughter. Babies in the nursery all join in a chorus of weeping when one baby begins to cry, and hardened criminals will find that their pulse rates go up at the sound of babies' wails. We laugh more heartily in a movie theater than when we are alone. We dance and drink in the company of others who raise (or lower) our spirits. Our happiness and depression are very much contributed to by our relations to others.

Indeed, we should more properly say that it takes a village to make someone depressed. First, you have to have a community define standards of what an individual should experience as normal. Is it normal to be sad or morose? Is it okay to be lethargic, or is the norm productivity, in which we work (if we can find a job) from nine to five for five or six days a week? Is sadness or extreme sadness something that is evoked by and evokes a communal interactivity? It is less and less possible, given the biological model, to see depression as a complex social phenomenon that defines standards and deviations from normal human behavior. Sociological, historical, and political analyses of depression have fallen to the wayside in favor of the individual's brain and its imbalances.

A stress-filled, distressing environment can provoke depression. Most people hate their jobs; the often-quoted statistic, true or not, is that one out of two marriages ends in divorce. Indeed, the event that most consistently triggers major sadness is the breakup of a marriage (which is also the theme of much popular music and the blues).[13] If a good deal of marriages end in divorce, we can imagine that a great many people will be distressed at some point in their lives, and add to that the death of a partner, another inevitable part of life, and you could double the number of those people. The majority of people in the United States are two or three paychecks away from homelessness. The median family income for the bottom 90 percent of Americans is $31,244. One out of ten adults are unemployed, and 16.5 percent of black adult males are without jobs. I could continue with such statistics, but the point is that there is not a lot to be happy about, and deep sadness and distress could well be the appropriate response to a world rife with inequality in which powerful forces control the lives of many citizens.

In this current era we don't like sociological explanations of depression. The preferred one, widely used and now considered absolute truth, is that depressed people have a chemical imbalance. The balance in question has to do with the level of serotonin in our brains. The argument goes that decreased serotonin makes us unhappy and that we need to correct that imbalance to make us return to equanimity if not outright happiness. In this sense, depression is a disease of the brain and only the brain—a disease that follows the hyper-hypo model of diabetes or thyroidism. In other words, there is a gradient continuum of a certain hormone or neurotransmitter, and too little of it creates a problem, as does too much (although in the case of serotonin, apparently you can't have too much).

But does this theory of brain-chemistry imbalance hold up to any scrutiny? Apparently not. There is no agreed-upon threshold or level of serotonin in the brain that makes you happy and below which you will be unhappy. Indeed, studies that lowered serotonin in the brain had no effect on depression. The authors of one such study wrote: "Although previously the monoamine systems [including serotonin] were considered to be responsible for the development of major depressive disorder (MDD), the available evidence to date does not support a direct causal relationship with MDD. There is no simple direct correlation of serotonin or norepinephrine levels in the brain and mood."[14] Some people with high levels of serotonin are unhappy, and there are those with a low level of serotonin who are happy. There is no way to measure brain serotonin short of cutting into the skull itself or doing so postmortem. Blood or spinal fluid serotonin levels are not necessarily correlated to brain levels, and one of the places of high serotonin levels in the body is in the gut, not the brain. As Jeffrey R. Lacasse and Jonathan Leo write:

> In short, there exists no rigorous corroboration of the serotonin theory, and a significant body of contradictory evidence. Far from being a radical line of thought, doubts about the serotonin hypothesis are well acknowledged by many researchers, including frank statements from prominent psychiatrists, some of whom are even enthusiastic proponents of SSRI medications. . . . However, in addition to what these authors say about serotonin, it is also important to look at what is not said in the scientific literature. To our knowledge, there is not a single peer-reviewed article that can be accurately cited to directly support claims of serotonin deficiency in any mental disorder, while there are many articles that present counterevidence.[15]

It is also not clear whether or not fiddling with one brain neurotransmitter will have adverse reactions on other neurotransmitters, since the brain, like the body, is based on a complex interaction among chemicals and an exquisitely delicate and self-regulating mechanism that belies the simplicity of the serotonin hypothesis. Indeed, even SSRIs are apparently not that selective. We have very little evidence that these supposedly targeted drugs are selective only for serotonin. Rather, there are ranges of neurotransmitters such drugs may affect.

I am not debunking the role of serotonin in depression just to be annoying. Rather, the foundation of the idea that depression is a biological problem rightly treated by physicians is based entirely on the argument that we know depression is a biological disease located in the brain because when serotonin (or any specific neurotransmitter) is low in humans, then depression results, and when it is raised, depression is cured. This is the capstone on the assertion that depression is a biological impairment and therefore a disability.

Given the putative assertion that chemical imbalances cause depression, is depression a medical disease? Many scholars have covered this ground, but I'll give a quick overview of the subject. To begin, let's agree that there exists psychic and emotional distress. This distress has been with us probably from the dawn of humanity and even before if we acknowledge that animals can experience pain that is not purely physical. Historically, such pain was not necessarily regarded as the purview of medicine. Indeed in the Renaissance and the Enlightenment, it was men of religion, not physicians, who often treated such psychic distress. Divines like Robert Burton, who wrote *The Anatomy of Melancholy,* and Dr. John Willis, who treated the madness of King George, were familiar figures in the treatment of emotional anguish. No one used the term *mental illness* until the nineteenth century, when the rise of the professionalization of medicine included a power grab by doctors to become the proprietors of the treatment and cure of what came to be called "mental illness." It's important to recall that the idea of illness implied that the causes of the disease were purely biological.

Medical articles like to state that depression has been around for centuries. But is that the case? You could say it has been around since antiquity, but in doing that you would have to be linking up earlier conceptions like *melancholia* to the term *depression.* But melancholia and depression aren't the same. Melancholia in the Middle Ages and the Renaissance involved seeing objects that were not there, as well as a physical state that was the result of an imbalance not of neurotransmitters but of humors. Melancholia might better be grouped under the current category of psychosis. But mainly melancholia was best known not as a disease so much as a personality type associated with the preponderance of certain humors. Aristotle wrote, "Why is it that all men who have become outstanding in philosophy, statesmanship, poetry or the arts are melancholic . . . ?"[16] In John Milton's poem "Il Penseroso" we see a type described rather than a diseased person. The speaker in the poem says that he would rather live with melancholia than with joy, which he sees as "vain [and] deluding."

> These pleasures Melancholy give,
> And I with thee will choose to live.

Melancholia, which literally means black-bile disorder, obviously stems from a Galenic humoral approach to the body, in which we no longer believe. But even our term *depression* has been readapted in the mid-twentieth century from the humoral explanation of health, in which there are animal "spirits" that circulate within the body. These "spirits" can be "high" or "depressed," and depressed spirits came to be "depression." The term *depression*, as separated from the idea of spirits and therefore in a psychological or psychiatric sense, is first recorded in the *OED* in 1905, although it was not used in our contemporary sense until the 1950s. In other words, modern depression is only about sixty years old.

From a cultural perspective we might want to consider that its current usage may have been linked in the minds of people in the 1950s to the historical event of the Great Depression, which had occurred only twenty years earlier and which carried vivid overtones of pain, suffering, and sadness within the culture. Indeed, one UK advertisement for an antidepressant from the early 1960s shows not the typical modern suburban housewife of most advertising, but a sad-looking woman in a Depression-era setting in front of a wood-burning stove in an obviously 1920s kitchen.[17] She herself is described as having been happily married for twenty-five years, which places her wedding in the Depression era.

The visual message may imply that depression ties one to the Great Depression. One might also want to consider that the antidepressants of choice in the 1950s and '60s were Miltown and Elavil, both of whose names convey the comfort of suburban development (both *town* and *ville*, evoking names like Levittown (the most famous development of the time) or Superboy's home Smallville, with its perfect American landscape, in opposition to the cultural memory of urban or rural squalor associated with the Great Depression. Prozac's advertising motto "Welcome Back!" echoes the nostalgia for a lost, perfect past, as well as Franklin Roosevelt's 1939 campaign song, "Back Again."

In short, with the rise of the psychiatric profession, sadness, a perfectly normal quality of humans, even perhaps from a poetic or artistic view a desired quality, came to be seen as a medical condition that needed cure and management by physicians. And that transformation of sorrow, sadness, and melancholy into the disease entity named "depression" came into being with the development of a new class of drugs first called "tranquilizers" and then, logically, "antidepressants"—both coined in the midpart of the twentieth century. It is also important to recall that before the pathologization of sadness, melancholia and later depression were considered major psychiatric conditions usually requiring hospitalization. But the new depression of the 1950s and 1960s was something that anyone might have, a mild to moderate sadness with a few other symptoms that in fact the majority of the population or a significant part of the population could experience.

In asking the question is depression a disease, we also have to include some ideas about how the disease is diagnosed. As previously cited, the *DSM* in its current form lists nine sets of symptoms; in order to be diagnosed with major depressive disorder (MDD), a person has to have five of the symptoms and to have had them for two weeks or more. Those symptoms include sadness, appetite loss or gain, insomnia, lethargy, suicidal thoughts, and so on. Bereavement is the only excluded form of sadness in the protocol, but excessive bereavement lasting more than two months is included.[18] What is clear from this description is that it is fairly easy to be diagnosed as having major depressive disorder if two weeks is the qualifying amount of time. In fact, it's hard to imagine being depressed for less than two weeks for many life-changing events. There is also the Hamilton Depression Rating Scale (HAM-D), which has been in use since the 1960s. People are rated on a number of factors like guilt, sleeplessness, restlessness, and so on. A friend of mine took it, not depressed by any obvious standards, and came up with a score of 18, the baseline for major depressive disorder. These biometric and symptomatic approaches lead one to see the socially constructed nature of the "disease" itself. In all cases, a diagnosis of mild to moderate depression or major depressive disorder will lead easily to treatment by SSRIs. Indeed, the focus of drug companies on alerting general practitioners to underlying depression almost guarantees that the quick fix at the level of family doctors will be a prescription for drugs rather than psychotherapy.

Before the development of antidepressants, there was not much interest in curing melancholia specifically. For one thing, very little was published on cure in the nineteenth and early twentieth centuries. Before then all that could be offered was what was offered for any "mental illness"—rest, baths, massage, good air, and healthful diet. These of course were offered for physical illnesses as well. Given that limited repertoire, it is interesting that Freud came along and became popular just when he did, because a "talking cure" seemed to offer a plan of treatment that differed from the expensive, time-consuming, and labor-intensive rest cures.

The first drugs used in the medical treatment of depression were barbiturates, stimulants in the amphetamine class, and lithium, the latter initially put in drinks like 7Up and White Rock sodas.[19] The general idea was that if the depression were caused by anxiety, a sedative would work; if lowered spirits caused it, then a stimulant would work. Neither of these drugs was considered specific to depression or any other condition but could act on and affect the mental state of any person taking the drug.

If the claim were that depression is a physical disease like a heart condition or an infectious disease, then one would assume the drug used to treat the disease would in effect cure it. It seems clear from the public record that far from curing depression, SSRIs are part of a big picture in which depression rates rise each year rather than diminish. As more and more people take SSRIs, more and more people are diagnosed as depressed. If *cure* is the wrong word, as drug company publicity suggests, perhaps depression is more like diabetes, which requires lifelong monitoring, maintenance, and care. But of course, this analogy falls down because there is no serotonin finger-prick device to monitor the levels of that neurotransmitter and no possibility of arriving at the normal level of serotonin required for happiness. The maintenance argument for depression is like saying that insomnia is the disease and Ambien cures it, or that headaches are cured by aspirin and therefore a lack of aspirin in the brain causes headache. No one would claim that sleeping pills cure insomnia, but rather they create symptoms that help one sleep longer. Therefore might we not say that alcohol or marijuana cures depression? Alcohol obviously has an effect on lifting the spirits, making the user less sad and increasing happiness.

Another key point is that SSRIs are not reliable drugs, as are insulin and sleeping pills. We know that an injection of insulin will lower blood sugar and that most people will experience drowsiness after taking a sleeping pill. But SSRIs are not reliable in that sense. Some people will be affected differently than other people, some people will not be affected at all, and some people will be affected positively, while others will be affected negatively. If Viagra had the same track record as Prozac, few men would use it.

Reliability is key for drugs, and so the analogy between SSRI therapy and insulin therapy is a poor one at best.

The word *drug* has the double sense of a substance taken to achieve a certain state of inebriation, distraction, stupefaction, or the like, as well as a chemical prescribed by a doctor to cure an illness. This double sense is elided particularly in the aura surrounding psychiatric drugs, which are seen only in the curative sense. But an important question to be raised here is how one tells the difference between a recreational drug (a misnomer because many people who take drugs do so to kill pain and numb anxiety; therefore addicts are not necessarily involved in a recreational activity) and a so-called pharmaceutical drug.

If your model is that depression is a disease, then taking a drug that cures the disease clearly is not a recreational activity, and the effects felt are thought to be the alleviation of the symptoms of the disease. If your model is that depression is a form of psychic distress, then taking a drug to dull the pain of being alive can be seen as an activity leading to addictive behavior. The distinction depends heavily on the model used but finally is a distinction without a difference. Using a model of biopower and control, we could speculate that drugs that make the person act in a way that is exuberant, uninhibited, and transgressive are considered recreational, while drugs that increase social control and restraint are considered therapeutic.

Another way of asking this question is: would you be a drug addict if you were taking a drug that raised your serotonin levels? Recent work on addiction, including the newest categorizations that were considered for the *DSM V*, conceives of addiction to shopping or sex as actually an addiction to the high felt when neuroreceptors are stimulated and produce increased amounts of, for example, dopamine, the "reward" neurotransmitter. So from this neurochemical point of view, activities themselves don't addict us, but rather we get addicted to the neurotransmitters produced by the activity. If that is the case, then why wouldn't taking a drug that increases serotonin, as SSRIs are touted as doing, be seen as addictive, since the goal is to increase the level of serotonin, as shopping might do for dopamine? The difference between Ecstasy (MDMA or 3,4-methylenedio xymethamphetamine) and an SSRI is a difference of mechanism only. One increases serotonin directly, and the other increases serotonin indirectly by decreasing the ability of the brain to metabolize the neurotransmitter. With Ecstasy we are dealing with a recreational drug, and with Prozac we are dealing with. . . . what?

Another aspect of the addictive issue is that addictive drugs are seen as bad because they are difficult to withdraw from. But, so the argument goes: SSRIs are not addictive, as might be barbiturates. However, the reality is that SSRIs are also very difficult to get off of. Users of the drugs frequently have very bad symptoms, including strong depression, nervousness, and sleeplessness, even suicide, as they taper off their use of the drugs. It's also unclear whether or not SSRIs have powerful effects of changing the brain itself, and so withdrawal will have even greater difficulties.

Even the concept of side effects, as Joanna Montcrief has pointed out, is a bit of a linguistic fudge—who is to say what are direct effects and what are side effects? Most SSRIs are tweaked versions of antihistamines and dyes.[20] Could an altered antihistamine or a modified version of methylene blue be said to have a main effect and then side effects? When you drink alcohol or smoke marijuana, what are the main effects and the side effects? Is the main effect intoxication and the side effect difficulty walking and slurred speech? The reality is that all drugs have a variety of effects. There may be ones you like and ones you don't, but the idea of side effects is simply ideological. The analogy might be to say that capitalism has its effects and its side effects. Depending on your social and economic situation, you might see the increasing gap between rich and poor as a side effect of stimulating the economy. Or you might see the gap as the main effect and the side effect as being the necessity to raise taxes on the majority of poorer wage earners. When we watch advertisements for drugs on television, we are made in both visual and auditory ways to experience the desired effect of the drug, usually seeing happy scenes of fulfilled and cured people and hearing in the voiceover a list of the devastating "side effects." The aim of the commercial is to make you feel that the visuals show the effect and the rapid voiceovers the unlikely other effects. But the reality is the drug might produce all, some, or none of the effects.

To recap, there is a problem with the disease model of psychic distress, and there is a problem with the drug "cure" for the disease model. In the former, we have medicalized a complex phenomenon with many symptoms grouped arbitrarily into a disease entity that we now call "depression." The drugs may have specific effects on some of those symptoms in ways that drugs work (uppers make you feel less lethargic, downers make you feel less nervous, added serotonin may make you feel less of both, or it may have no effect on you at all).

If we discuss the effectiveness of SSRIs, we get into another complex discussion. When Prozac first came on the scene in the 1990s, there was virtually universal acclaim for it, despite the fact that it had been kicking around looking for a use since the 1950s. Popular books like Peter Kramer's *Listening to Prozac* and many self-help books told the stories of how effective these drugs were and how they selectively increased serotonin (neither claim is true). So did many articles in prominent journals that recounted randomized clinical trials (RCTs) in which SSRIs appeared to be at least 70 percent effective. In the initial excitement of the 1990s, the use of these drugs filtered quickly down to the prescription pads of general practitioners, who prescribed SSRIs with abandon. In addition to SSRIs being prescribed for depression, a host of other conditions, including anxiety, obsessive-compulsive disorder (OCD), and many new conditions, were developed as off-uses of the drugs—"diseases" like situational affective disorder, parental defiance disorder, and so on. SSRIs began to be used widely on children, although no studies had been done on the safety of this usage for developing brains.

In the following years, with the excitement of prescribing these "new" drugs waning and with more information emerging about suppressed studies and new clinical trials, the effectiveness of these drugs was found to be in the range of a placebo, either below or slightly above. So instead of 70 percent effectiveness, we are now getting the picture of SSRIs being about 33 percent effective. Research has shown that major drug companies initially suppressed the results of trials that showed this class of medication to be much less effective than the 70 percent they aimed to tout.[21] Further, drug companies ghostwrote articles for authorities in the field who then published them under their own names in the most visible and well-known journals. These articles then were themselves reprinted and publicized. There currently is a debate going on concerning the validity of all the randomized clinical trials and the roundup articles that look at such trials. Those who have supported SSRIs all along claim that the new studies and the reevaluation of old studies showing the barely effective nature of these drugs are invalid for a variety of reasons. Those who question the effectiveness of these drugs, on the other hand, now have a lot of clinical and research data to make the case otherwise. Irving Kirsch, who has published some of the definitive work reexamining clinical trials, has written that "my colleagues and I were led to the inescapable conclusion that antidepressants are little more than active placebos."[22]

Given what I've summarized, it would seem that a good case can be made that depression is not a medical disease and, although biologically based, in the sense that so many of our functions are located in the brain, is not cured by SSRIs. Peter Kramer has an interesting way of putting this problematic—if depression is a disease, should we (if we had a magic wand and could) wipe it out as we did smallpox?[23] There are few people who would advocate such an eradication since by doing so we would very much change what it means to be human—including the influence of depression on the arts, culture, and daily life. In fact, Kirsch suggests that we might better think of depression not as a disease, but as a normal function of human neurochemistry and neuroanatomy: "Depression may result from a normally functioning brain, containing neural networks that have been shaped by life events and that respond to current life demands in a way that is experienced subjectively as sadness and despair. It may be the events themselves that make us feel lost and hopeless, or it may be the way in which we have learned to interpret those events. In either case, the underlying brain mechanisms may be normal."[24] Kirsch suggests that the normal functions of the brain might include feedback loops with the outer world. In other words, depression is part of the normal function of the brain in the context of learned patterns and real-world exigencies.

If mild to moderate depression isn't a disease and SSRIs don't work as anything more than an active placebo, then why do so many people and their medical practitioners report positive effects from taking this class of drugs? And should we discount what they say simply because the clinical trials don't support the idea that SSRIs actually work? In writing this chapter and speaking about the subject, I have found many people who rigorously maintain that they are medically depressed and have been helped vastly by SSRIs. They don't really care about the science, the academic argument, or the qualifications. SSRIs worked for them. From the patient's point of view it goes like this: if I take this drug and it works for me, what is wrong with that? And from the physician's point of view: I don't really care if the serotonin hypothesis is wrong; it provides a simple explanation that allows patients to take a drug that will help them without feeling guilty and responsible for their condition.

Involved in the "works for me" approach are the many people who take SSRIs and respond with their own narratives. These personal narratives, in print and online, are very compelling, although they cut both ways. Some people report life-saving effects and relief from personal suffering from taking SSRIs. Other people report devastating "side" effects, including suicidal impulses and the actual suicides of relatives or friends. Indeed, one of the findings is that SSRIs, particularly when given to young adults, lead to increased suicide rates for those taking the drug, and current warnings now include screening advice to physicians alerting them to these dangers for adolescents. Other significant effects of the drug are loss of sexual interest, digestive and sleep problems, depression itself, muscle twitches, agitation, and many other discomforts. While we are very interested in the development of narrative medicine and in the distinction between disease and illness (the objective pathology and the patient's experience of being ill), it is hard to base policy decisions and political ones solely on individual claims. "Works for me" is of course the argument that can never be opposed, since who can deny someone's claim of personal benefit? But in the past a whole range of medical cures "worked for me" for many people. Let us say simply that "works for me" has nothing to do with scientific knowledge and is more akin to the many personal experiments we make in the course of our lives, from deciding that peanut butter works for you to deciding that almond butter doesn't. These are valid choices always, but not discussable in regard to general knowledge and policy.

It might be that the only alternative to the "works for me" argument is double-blind, randomized clinical trials. It is possible, however, to argue that the very nature of such trials is problematic when dealing with grab-bag diagnoses like depression. If what we have said is true—that what we call depression is actually a collection of symptoms that might be grouped in other ways and have been at various other historical periods—then clinical trials might not make sense since there is no discrete disease entity to be studied. If it is also true that it takes a village to make a psychological disease—since one's level of happiness or sadness is often culturally determined—then clinical trials might be looking at the wrong thing. If one's sense of responsibility for sadness or depression is a result of a shared community of values and feelings, then is depression a discrete illness? If we can say that depression is not a discrete entity but one arrived at in complex ways, then can a clinical trial be run on something that amorphous? Also, it is hard to say what constitutes cure. What kind of measures will reflect improvement or backsliding? Can we come up with meaningful benchmarks?

On the other hand, if we don't have clinical trials, what do we have? Clinical trials are a haphazard and imprecise way to measure whether a drug is working in the way that its manufacturers claim it is working. The alternative is the physician's equivalent of "works for me." When huge amounts of money are at stake, as well as health and governmental policy, the functioning of large institutions, and enormous profits for big pharma, can we rely on anecdotal evidence alone?

While I recognize the dubious nature of trying to run clinical trials on disease entities that shift and change every thirty years, I still think that we need to pay attention not so much to RCTs as to the analyses of multiple RCTs. Kirsch shows that virtually all trials of depression drugs yield the same numbers and the same results when assessed in meta-analyses.[25]

Thus far I have been discussing the issue of disability and a disease and the lock-step argument that depression is a disease because it responds to drugs. But the whole issue of the disease-drug model is in some sense yesterday's news. The current thinking is more and more that depression isn't so much a problem of chemical imbalance as it is a problem of brain anatomy and genetics. With the advent of PET and fMRI scans, we appear to have the ability to watch the brain at work. That and forensic studies allow neuroscientists to locate areas of the brain and see if they are involved in depression. Much of that work is ongoing, and it may well have an important role to play in explaining how depression functions in the brain. What we can say is that these studies are still in the early phases of helping us understand the vastly complex way the brain works. Early studies will have to be confirmed and repeated before we can say that one theory or one location is involved. As with OCD and a host of other mental disorders, theoretical problems remain in this realm of study. First, brain-scan devices, while promising, are still very crude. Rather than finding specific locations in the brain, which these machines do, what seems key to the complexity of the brain are actually neural networks, and the current scanners we have can't trace those accurately and precisely. Perhaps the next generation of scanners will be able to trace more accurately what is happening in the brain. Second, we don't really have the ability to link the serotonin hypothesis to brain anatomy with any reliability since we can't see or measure monoamines like dopamine or serotonin with brain scans; all we can do is measure blood flow or oxidation. So far we don't have agreement on locations in the brain that control depression—a host of locations are suspect, the frontal lobes, the temporal lobes, the hippocampus, the amygdala, the hypothalamus, the suprachiasmatic nucleus, and the other usual suspects from central brain casting that show up in a range of studies including obsessive-compulsive disorder and a host of other conditions. And finally, there is the same question we have with chemical theories—is depression a discrete disease or a collection of symptoms? If the latter, then we will have to find a variety of explanations for each symptom—sleeplessness may be located in one location, lethargy in another, and rumination in another.

Adding to the difficulty of the new research is the study of genetic causes. While there are indications that depression is inherited to some degree, there have not been any definitive findings of the mechanism of genetic inheritance. As will probably be the case, the genetic causes will be multiple and varied, and there will be difficulty mapping the genetic discoveries onto the serotonin theories and the brain-anatomy theories. In any case, we are very far from any grand unified theory of the biological causes of depression. And to complicate genetics further, we are now seeing that genes aren't the final determinant since environment is crucial to the way genes and epigenetic factors interact. Complex feedback loops between the environment and gene expression make each person and each haplotype group experience the interaction of multiple factors in different ways. It's pretty clear that a single gene or set of genes will have limited involvement, at best, in explaining the genesis of depression. As Peter Kramer has written, "genes and experience are thoroughly mingled."[26]

What does all this have to do with disability? I think there are profound questions raised by such a consideration of depression. I would begin with an obvious one: depression is based on a medical model. According to the World Health Organization (WHO), depression will be the second leading cause of disability in the world by 2020, exceeded only by heart disease. The organization estimates that depression is the leading cause of disability for fifteen- to forty-four-year-olds.[27] What I am arguing for, along with others, is a careful rethinking of the value of the biologically based model in areas of psychic distress such as depression, anxiety, obsessive-compulsive disorder, and the like. It is not at all clear that the medical model is adequate to the complexity of these states of mind, heart, and being. It is also not clear that the medical model even has any validity when scrutinized. Certainly, at least, one could say that the medical explanations range from assumption, to premise, to misconception. And the least we can say is that there is ongoing controversy and disagreement even within the medical profession on the diagnosis and treatment of such disorders.

Given that depression is framed and treated within a medical model as a biological disease, what could a social model, the central tenet of disability studies, have to say about this framing of sorrow and sadness as pathology? The social model, which sees that there are biologically based impairments, asserts that these only become disabilities in a disabling society. There are of course benefits and pitfalls to using a medical model to describe an affective and cognitive phenomenon. The upside is that the individual can no longer be considered responsible for his or her mental or emotional state. In the past it used to be that the individual or the parents of the individual were in some sense responsible for the condition. If you were depressed, it was because of some choices you made in the past or your personal way of handling difficult or challenging moments in your history. And if you weren't responsible, then a domineering mother or a passive father might have been. With the biological model, all of that responsibility goes out the window, and it is your genes or your homeostatic chemical system that is the culprit. Strangely, it used to be that saying you had a brain disease was a stigma, but with the chemical imbalance/serotonin hypothesis, the stigma is virtually gone. The downside of the medical model is that it involves taking pharmaceuticals as the main current treatment. The issue of responsibility shifts from those who supposedly caused the disease to the individual. Now you are pressured by friends, family, and partners as well as the general culture to take the drug and take it for years, if not forever. It is your responsibility to remember to take the drugs, not to lapse, and to continue to keep switching drugs to find one that will work after the efficacy of the drug you are currently taking begins to attenuate. It is also your responsibility to tolerate the "side effects" and to take further drugs to reduce those effects. In other words, instead of thinking of society as accommodating your disability, it is actually you who has to accommodate society.

Another issue to consider is that of normality. As I've written,[28] the rise of the idea of normality is intimately linked to the rise of the concept of the abnormal and of the correction of abnormalities in the human race through eugenic strategies. There is thus a very strong eugenic influence when one talks about the normal, particularly as it applies to the body and to the mind. In disability studies we look with suspicion on arguments that rely on the normal functioning of the physical, the cognitive, and the affective. So when we come to think about the normal state of humans, we might want to be equally suspicious about ideas of normal happiness and what constitutes abnormal sorrow. Indeed, as Horowitz and Wakefield[29] point out, there has developed a slippage of the term *normal*, which used to apply to the normal sorrows that accompany loss.[30] The new normal excludes that kind of sorrow and pain from everyday life and imagines a revised standard in which humans are happy all the time. This new abnormal includes what used to be considered quite normal—major sadness at the breakup of a marriage, the loss of a job, and the many other disappointments of life. In effect, the new definition of depression, so broad as to include 25 percent of the world, according to WHO, creates a new form of what might be called "psychosocial eugenics." We are no longer necessarily trying to breed a better human, but we are trying to enforce through diagnosis and chemical intervention a new, more perfect emotional life. Sadness, sorrow, and pain have little room in that brave new world.

Disability studies has promoted the idea that it is not the individual who has the disability, but society at large that creates disabling barriers and a lack of accommodation. With the medical model, it is only the individual who "has" depression. But if what we are saying is that it takes a village to create a depressed person, then the lone disease-ridden person is a kind of fiction invented by medicine and fostered by drug companies. Is it the case, then, that everyone is just a diagnosis and a pill away from disability? It's hard to see how this particular medical model of depression would map nicely onto a social model. In fact, the medical model, as we might expect, contradicts the social model. Worse, the only accommodation presented by the medical model is increasingly lifelong drug use. Granted, there is no longer a major stigma around being depressed, so some of the discrimination we have seen historically against "mentally ill" people has been reduced or at least attenuated with the chemical-imbalance model. But the disability is definitely residing in the person, or more specifically in the person's chemistry. And the element of social control is much stronger— one is obliged to go on drugs and rallied to do so by partners, family, and friends.

Another fundamental tenet of the social model of disability studies is the distinction between impairment and disability. The classic example illustrating this concept is that of the paraplegic who uses a wheelchair. In so doing, that person is not mobility impaired as long as he or she is in an environment with ramps and elevators. With physical disabilities, the diagnosis of the impairment is usually straightforward and obvious, as is the political and social remedy—ramps, curb cuts, and elevators. But with psychic distress, the diagnoses can vary, symptoms can shift, and cures are not always obviously the same. Even the categories and epistemology of such diseases are not clear and shift from decade to decade. So the impairment diagnosis itself is not exempt from the forces of social construction and ideological control. The most compelling question to ask is: which is more disabling—the attitude of society toward depression or the construction of the disease entity itself? In the case of the legless woman, society's attitude constitutes a major part of what is disabling about the impairment. But with depression, society has become quite accepting of people who are depressed (as long as they are taking drugs).[31] So the major harm does not seem to come in job discrimination, social ostracizing, or other kinds of stigma. Rather the disabling, I would argue, comes from the genealogy of the disease entity, its association with medical diseases, and the major effects of the drugs taken.

The medicalization of emotional states, I am saying, is a disabling move. Think of the change that occurs in our way of thinking of, for example, literary characters if we medicalize them. Eeyore, of course, would not longer be sad all the time; he'd have major clinical depression caused by a chemical imbalance, as would Hamlet. Holden Caulfield would have oppositional defiance disorder. Fanny Price would have situational affective disorder. Scrooge would have obsessive-compulsive personality disorder, and David Copperfield would have parental alienation disorder. All of them would go on SSRIs immediately. The rich brew of their lives as narrated by their authors would dissolve into a diagnosis, and their salvation would be written on a prescription pad.

While this is just a thought experiment, perhaps it highlights what happens as we proceed in this century, revising the *DSM* accordingly, to a society in which personality traits and emotional reactions are increasingly seen as pathological states. The end goal would be that most of the population would have SSRIs or some related drug coursing through their blood as mega amounts of money flowed from individuals to big pharma corporations. Given that health care is the largest sector of our economy, a considerable portion of that economy would be devoted to this form of social organization. The disablement involved is one in which valuable resources will flow from the many to the few, increasing the gap between the 1 percent and the 99 percent.

In the mid-twentieth century there were dystopic visions of the future in which all members of a society were on drugs. But even in *Brave New World*, where the drug *Soma*[32] is used, it is only taken occasionally as a cheap and efficient vacation from the cares of the daily world. The vision of the Soviet use of drugs and forced treatment of mental illness as a proxy for imprisonment of political dissidents was prevalent in the 1960s, and films like *One Flew Over the Cuckoo's Nest* presented incarceration of the normal achieved through neuroleptic drugs, forced shock treatment, and involuntary commitment. But none of those scenarios gave us the moment we have now. In terms of biopower, as described by Michel Foucault, we are living in a time when people are "voluntarily" putting themselves on drug regimens in numbers that would have been unimaginable in the past. It is hard to accede to the fact that such a situation is not disabling. Indeed, psychological impairments are being created at an exponential rate. with the *DSM* adding new illnesses at each printing at a rate of 25 percent.

On the other hand, one of the principles of disability studies and of what I am calling "dismodernism" is that the future should expand to allow the seamless interface of the prosthetic and the human. The old distinction between human and machine collapses as interconnectivity through the Internet and digital technologies changes the nature of life and perception. Also, the claim that there is a natural body is being debunked by the options of cosmetic surgery and gender reassignment, the latter using hormones to reshape and redesign the birth body. Don't we now see transgendered people who are transitioning by using hormones over the course of a life as a parallel to individuals committed to the lifelong use of SSRIs? So why not consider depressed people who are transitioning to happy people as analogous to the transgender model? Why should we not consider someone on a lifelong drug regime to cure depression as a person using a chemical prosthesis?

Perhaps the issue is the extent to which any given state is rendered abject and marginal by biopower in the context of neoliberalism (or any other form of state power). So if being female is seen as being a second-class citizen, then transitioning from a female to a male may well be an act of self-actualization, but it is also one that cannot escape the political and social valence of masculinity over femininity. Likewise, if a society values independence, productivity, energy, and being upbeat over inertia, lethargy, sadness, and enervation, then the desire to take SSRIs is not a free and clear choice.

The issue of disability then becomes somewhat vexed because the notion of a prosthesis that remedies an impairment is doubly muddled. The first muddle is whether depression is a disease at all and therefore is actually an impairment. And it is muddled again because it is not clear that a lifelong drug effect is prosthetic or simply something else. A drug would be a prosthesis if it restored or imitated some primary state that appears to be natural and useful. This would presume that happiness and well-being were aspects of this primary state. In neoliberal society the assumption is that middle-class life, rife with consumer objects and now with digital interconnectivity, will be happy. As we socially network, we post positive and humorous comments so the world can see our kids, our cats, and us in this best light. But if this well-being and happiness is not a primary state but a fictional and posited condition, a condition that is the sine qua non of the globalized, cosmopolitan, postmodern existence, then are we still talking about these drugs as prostheses, or are they more appropriately thought of as requirements for admission to this imaginary class of beings? In the same way that working-class people often might think that if they imitate the clothing or lifestyles of the rich and famous they will be able to affect their attitude toward their own class status, do people who take drugs to be happy ally themselves with the regnant ideological demands of their nation and era? Class is much more durable than a change of clothing, and likewise the state of happiness pictured as part of the neoliberal lifestyle is something that you can't buy or take in a pill form.

I recognize that if read incorrectly, I seem to be doing no more in this chapter than decrying modern life and the accoutrements of a bourgeois lifestyle. I don't want to be Jeremiah, and less do I want this work to be a jeremiad. Nor do I want to be Cassandra, seeing the collapse of some imagined past harmonious and balanced society in the present future. But what I am pointing to is that a disability studies approach to depression and SSRIs might produce a different and stronger argument than the run-of-the-mill broken-brain model.

In the broken-brain model, a chemical imbalance causes depression or an anomaly in brain physiology, which can be cured by the taking of SS-RIs. This approach, according to Joanna Moncrieff, is itself disabling: "The idea that your emotional state has been caused by a biochemical imbalance in your brain is profoundly disempowering. . . . [People taking SSRIs] are not likely to recognize the things that they did to help themselves out of depression. . . . If in contrast they had managed to get through the period without taking a drug . . . they would have had an experience of self-efficacy that could build their confidence and help them face future problems with greater strength."[33] Thus the SSRI approach "conveys a message of hopelessness and powerlessness."[34]

The construction of psychiatric disorders can be empowering or disempowering. As with the case of drapetomania, a disease identified by the American physician Samuel Cartright in the nineteenth century that caused African American slaves to want to run away and be free, we now can easily see the obvious ideological and disempowering aspect of such a diagnosis. And the medical cures suggested for drapetomania, including whipping, would be difficult to imagine as prosthetic or curative in any contemporary sense. Also consider neurasthenia, a disease thought to result from the speed and stress of modern life, particularly affecting women who wanted to work, which was widely diagnosed and required specific cure in the nineteenth and twentieth centuries. These "diseases" are now widely regarded as ideologically constructed disorders, but we could equally see depression as following the august line of such conditions, which made sense at the time and later did not.

The arc of the narrative structure of depression stories—both self-help books and memoirs—inevitably includes the "overcoming" story. People in disability studies have learned to be suspicious of this paradigm because it seems to be one of the master plots of an ableist culture. Nondisabled people apparently can't get enough of this narrative fix, but those of us in disability studies look cautiously at any disability whose narrative turn automatically follows this pattern. If we see depression as a disease, and one that creates suffering in the narrator, then we will want the narrator to overcome the disease and cure it, thus applying the medical model to a psychological condition. If depression is the result of a biological fact—a chemical imbalance—then the application of drugs to cure this disease is the way to go. And the narrative arc from disabled to cured is the satisfying one for readers of books like Andrew Solomon's *The Noonday Demon* or Meri Nana-Ama Danquah's *Willow Weep for Me: A Black Woman's Journey through Depression* (the latter seems to have been supported by Eli Lilly, manufacturer of Zoloft,[35] whose executive director interviews Danquah at the end of the book and which sponsored publicity and a road tour for the book).[36]

If we were mindful of a disability paradigm, then we would want to consider the value of certain disabilities and think twice about the overcoming story. For example, people involved in the Icarus Project see conditions like depression or bipolar disorder as "mad gifts needing cultivation and care, rather than diseases or disorders."[37] Since so many artists and creative people are bipolar or experience the symptoms of depression, the Icarus Project sees its job as helping people navigate the space between "brilliance and madness." Organizations like Mad Pride and Mindfreedom.org "celebrate the human rights and spectacular culture of people considered very different by our society."[38] At the end of the day, our approach to depression can be seen as a political act rather than only a medical one. There are probably advantages to each, but the political stance is one that empowers, while the other is one that labels.

Perhaps what we need in place of overcoming-depression stories and the worldwide web of drugs is some sense of what we might call "depression pride," promulgated by the Icarus Project and others. Kay Redfield Jamison, in her memoir *An Unquiet Mind*, asks herself at the end of the book whether she would rather be free of depression. She writes: "I honestly believe that as a result of it I have felt more things, more deeply; had more experiences, more intensely; loved more, and have been more loved; laughed more often for having cried more often."[39] She goes on with a long list of positives.

If we were back in the bad old days of rampant ableism, many people would, as many even now still do, think of a disability as a negative, something worse than death. While I don't want to downplay the difficulties and pain of acute sadness and despair, and I don't want to minimize the pain and difficulty of having impairments in general, the overall message of disability studies is that there is a bright side, a very bright side, to being a person with a disability. Why cannot we shine that brightness onto the darkness of depression?

Irving Kirsch notes that the thing about depression is that it is depressing. It is a state by definition without hope. Kirsch says that drugs (and placebos) give the person without hope some hope. [40]And that hope can move the depressed person out of the slough of despair. But if placebos, St. John's Wort, cognitive behavioral therapy, and exercise[41] can all produce results as good as SSRIs, perhaps a shift in social attitudes can help as well.[42] If depression is seen as a "dangerous gift," as the Icarus Project puts it, if depression pride can be promulgated along with the other identity prides, then perhaps there are more routes out of the abyss than the relatively rickety and dangerous ladder offered by the disease model and its chemical cures.

CHAPTER FIVE

Stumped by Genes

DNA, Disability, and Prosthesis

A new field of thought is emerging that, for want of a better term, is being called *biocultures*—the study of the scientificized and medicalized body in history, culture, and politics. Biocultural approaches have been used to explore various kinds of phenomena from the out-of-boundary[1] disciplines of the humanities, social sciences, medical sciences, and so on. Biocultural analysis is to these discourses as theory has been to the humanistic discourses. In this chapter, I take a biocultural approach to examining genetics and use this culture-based way of knowing to look at certain issues in the field of genetic and medical research.

One notion of prosthesis approaches genetics through a reconceptualization of the idea of prosthesis that is permeable to medical and technological ways of thinking and to linguistic- and humanities-oriented ways of knowing. This type of analysis might begin with the observation that the original meaning of *prosthesis* in English is "addition," notably first used not in a physiological or technological sense, but in a grammatical one as an element that is *added* to a sentence. This original grammatical meaning is transformed at the end of the eighteenth century into a medical meaning—something that is *added* in surgery. The comfortable continuation between science and the humanities was very much a sign of those times; in today's science-self-segregated world, a jump between the two disciplines would be harder to make. The meaning of *prosthesis* as something that is added to the body becomes much more widely used in the middle and late nineteenth century, when it comes to mean, fairly exclusively, an artificial limb or part that supplements the original but missing body part.

According to the *Oxford English Dictionary*, *prosthesis* as a supplement to grammar or parts of speech is connected to *prosthesis* as a supplement to body parts. As Jacques Derrida's work on Jean-Jacques Rousseau and the supplement has shown, Rousseau's famous "Essay on the Origin of Language" took late-eighteenth-century readers into an inquiry about the way that human language develops. In looking at Rousseau, Derrida develops a theory of the "supplement." He notices that Rousseau opposes nature and society and sees the latter as a supplement of nature. Rousseau, according to Derrida, privileges nature and fits it into a series of oppositions, including health and disease, purity and contamination, good and evil, and speech and writing.

By this privileging of nature, language can be thought about as a supplement—something prosthetic that is added to nature rather than being of nature itself. Spoken language, according to Rousseau, is closer to nature than written language, which is further away from the natural origin of words. Derrida's theory is in opposition, for example, to Noam Chomsky's notion of language as inherently part of human nature—as hardwired into the brain and therefore not a prosthetic. So being human becomes an aspect of supplementarity. Humans are not natural because language, at least written language, is a supplement.

Theses oppositions can be seen as defining a new set of expectations about what is human and how the human animal fits into the biosphere—the anthropocene world that is inhabited by and made habitable (or inhabitable) by the human animal. This ambiguity also can be found in the original disability-related notion of prosthetics in the word *stump*, a word that refers to both the part of body that remains and the prosthetic that replaces what is missing. The stump of a limb is replaced by a wooden leg, also referred to as a stump. The cut-down root of a tree is a stump, and by analogy the limb that is removed from the body is also a stump. Ironically, the wooden leg participates in the original sin of the removal by being part of the metaphoric and metonymic tree so that the human gains a stump from the stump created in the tree. The analogies continue as one is foiled by tripping on a stump and then comes to be stumped by the difficulty of the tree and by the stomping sound made by the stump leg, which combines the fleshly stump with the wooden stump.

The prosthetics industry in the nineteenth century got its jump-start following the Civil War in the United States, a war in which more American soldiers died than in all other US wars combined. Massive numbers of men perished, and massive numbers survived—many of them maimed.

Nascent industry saw that restoring the wholeness of the divided country was achievable, again through metaphor and metonym, by restoring the limbs of soldiers who had given part of their bodies so that their country's body would remain whole and undivided. The call to return all amputees to working citizenship found its answer in the technological and cosmetic enhancement of the artificial limb. But why after the Civil War did prosthetics manufacturers begin making realistic-looking limbs rather than the wooden stumps that had been widely used before? Was this a result of a general eugenic push that promoted the normal and tried to exorcise the abnormal? Was there a sense that amputees had to appear distinctly normal—to fake normality (itself a contradictory state)?

This question has stumped researchers in the history of prosthetics. In a sense, its answer involves the supplementary notion of the prosthetic difference as both addition and removal. A new biocultural history of prosthetics might involve this ambiguity as well since it is built into the idea of the prosthetic. The issues involve the metaphorics of limb replacement and the complex contradictions that are embodied in the removal of the body part and the replacement with the supplement.

Another way of thinking about prosthesis considers the issue of a kind of bodily surplus value in which the work of replacement takes value from the worker, the manufacturer, and also the body that is being prostheticized. What loss comes from the gain? What value is added and, in the same process, diminished in the addition?

Rather than trace a material history of prosthetics in this manner, which would be a perfectly good endeavor, I want to shift the ground a bit for the purposes of this chapter and consider the outcome of the prosthetic difference—the notion of supplementarity in the discussion around genetics and race. The word *prosthetics* is not used much in this context but seems to me to inform the discussion by providing a milieu of replacement and supplementarity to notions of being human.

The ambiguity around the notion of "genetic" in one sense comes from an active generation or genesis involved in human reproduction. Genetic is both an active notion and a passive one. The activeness of generating physical and physiological changes occurs through a genetic activity and a passive activity in the sense that the genetic is seen as fixed and written, like a written language. The opposition between spoken and written language plays out in the modern conception of genetics that contains both the vocalized natural (thus subject to change and self-making) and the fixed, inscribed, written-in-stone sense of genetic fate or destiny. In addition, the ambiguity of the real-looking but actually "fake" prosthetic limb is now eliminated in the genetic era with DNA of genes appearing totally "fake" in the popular imagination and known by computer-graphic representations (the double helix with colored bits representing the "building blocks"). Yet genes are presumed to be natural and "in" the body, part of the body, in a way that "real-looking" artificial limbs can never be.

The areas in which some of these ideas of fixity and mutability played themselves out were in notions of race, degeneracy, and the human body. In the nineteenth century, race was developed as a "scientific" concept—first along phenotypic lines, as a measurable, quantifiable categorization of human populations. Brain size, hair color, type, skin color, and so on were measured and charted. In this sense, race was seen as inherently part of the human body—in no way prosthetic. Yet this quiddity of race, its fixity in the body, also contained notions of change. The human body over generations, and even within one single body, could change, improve, or degenerate. In fact, the mechanisms of race were poorly theorized. For example, it was believed that racial characteristics would diminish over several generations, yet it was also believed that race was strong enough to survive even if people had only one grandparent of a particular race.

The mode of transmission for race was conceived as occurring through some idea of transmission of racialized blood. Because notions of inheritance were poorly understood, perceived hereditary conditions, like race, were seen almost as disease entities passed along over generations by an improbable combination of mixing of blood, Lamarckian adaptation, and general influences. When Gregor Mendel made public his work on garden peas, the first steps were taken toward a more scientific explanation of inheritance. However, most people do not realize that Mendel's ideas were mathematical only and did not advance any clear notion of what genes were or how they worked. Mendel merely told the world about the distribution of certain traits—how likely a specific trait was to appear in offspring. In fact, the idea of the gene is itself a kind of cobbling together of Mendel's notion of the distribution of traits with another notion that there had to be a place that traits could call home—the gene. Based on the relatively flawed idea that a single factor is responsible for a single trait, Mendel's work was nevertheless influential. Although Mendel did not call that "place" a gene, he left open the idea that the gene, in this sense, is a prosthesis—a human-conceived artifact that stands in for, replaces, and thus becomes the location of the inherited traits. In fact, the "realness" of the gene in the current discourse is belied by the fact that there really was no locus—no "there"

there—for genes. So the prosthetic gene was in fact an imaginary location that replaced the "realness" of physical features, hair color, and so on.

Aside from the strides that Mendel made in his mathematical formula, very little serious work followed on the actual way that traits were inherited. It was not until the 1950s, when James Watson and Francis Crick discovered the chemical structure of DNA, that an actual mechanism for inheritance was hypothesized on a chemical and molecular basis. Here again, it is necessary to have a prosthetic understanding of what it was that Watson and Crick "discovered." Their discovery was that DNA had the structure of the double helix (although recent work has led to some questioning of whether they did indeed "discover" this information or simply ended up explaining in detail what other scientists at the time had already discovered).

Indeed, Watson and Crick did not discover the gene, although we still use this term to describe the prosthetic space of inheritance. They discovered the mechanism by which DNA replicates itself. The gene remains in fact a semi-fictional entity without an existence. There really is no gene as a locatable place or item, and science tends to use the term as a kind of prosthesis to mark the place where the location of the gene should be if there were a gene. What we do have is a continuous stretch of nucleotides over which we draw a set of limits. The gene, like the prosthetic leg, marks the place of an absence and acts as a physical memorial to something lost. What was lost, in fact, was the certainty that race was real, had a location, was "there." The gene now acts as a kind of prosthetic *en abime*, an endlessly deferred location. In this sense, like grammatical usage and the "real-looking" fake limb, the gene has come to take the place of something else that in many ways cannot be named. We can call it the place of the certainty of race. In the early years of genetic thinking, the gene essentially took the place of—was the prosthetic for—the idea of racialized phenotypes. Yoked to eugenic concepts and notions of inheritance, the gene came to do the work of race. If "Negroid" people had kinky hair and flat noses, the there had to be a gene for each trait. If Jews were labeled degenerate, then the gene was the location for their flat feet, nervousness, feeblemindedness, and so on. While the term *eugenics* was discarded by the 1930s, the replacement term for the same endeavor was *genetics*. Indeed, the now-infamous center for eugenics at Cold Spring Harbor, New York, became by a simple name change the new national center for genetics. In London, the Eugenics Society changed its name to the more neutral Galton Institute, named after Sir Francis Galton, the founder of eugenics.

In other words, the gene was the prosthetic location for traits that were presumed to be real and verifiable—but that location had never been seen or even ascertained by any other means. The gene was a virtual prosthetic—a location like heaven that had to exist if there were a Christian God, as the gene had to exist if there were inheritable traits. The human body, as a construct, could not have an entirety and an identity if there were no addition, now called genetic, that was the place of origin, the real place for being human and for being a certain kind of human—whether "Caucasian" or "Negroid" or "Semitic."

Because genetics is both a research area and an area of biotechnology with an elaborated and scientific discourse surrounding it, nonscientists tend to assume that all is well and well organized in this world. But a biocultural approach can provide various kinds of illuminations and insights that are not always available to a scientific one. To achieve these interventions, we need to inform ourselves about the science associated with genetics. Thus, common knowledge and journalistic explication posits a "gene" for language, depression, intelligence, breast cancer, even gayness or deafness. What needs to be made clear here is that complex human processes cannot be contained in a single gene for several reasons. First, a gene is not an actual place or thing. Second, one gene is supposed to make one protein. Complex human processes like intelligence can never be the result of the production or lack of production of a single protein. We can say that the idea of the gene for a complex trait is a prosthetic that posits the trait as an addition to being human. Thus the default gene for humans is, say, heteronormative activity, and the prosthetic, added on to this, replacing the normative gene, is homosexuality. In this sense, the original is what is actually socially constructed as belonging to the body; the replacement part is seen as inferior, as a wooden leg would be considered "not as good" or "not as real looking" as the original one of flesh.[2] We could construct a series of such prosthetics that are seen as "add-ons" to all the major categories of otherness in dominant, medicalized culture. Thus blackness would be the prosthesis for the whiteness, femininity for masculinity, and so on.

What I am getting at is that even though there may be good, even the best, science behind genetics, the level of science gets one only so far in a social, cultural context—the context in which we live. The next stage—the biocultural stage in which science interacts with the biosphere, the mental, the physical, ideological, architectural space—is always going to have to rely on imaginings, which will lead us to various ways of metaphorizing the explanatory system (in this case, genetics). Are genes *in* the body, *of* the body, or *in addition to* the body? Science seems not to deal in meanings or significations and claims to present an unmediated reality, but the idea of the gene—the idea of the double helix, as we visualize it, the idea of the direct connection among allele, DNA, RNA, protein—is a complicated one that exists in a frame of meanings and significations. To fully imagine the facts requires a biocultural understanding that is only just developing in both the sciences and the humanities. Thus, even on the level of the greatest degrees of hypersignification, a kind of intellectual supplementation—indeed, prosthesis—is required to understand all the parameters in the play of meanings and facts that are inherent in the genetic gamble being undertaken at the present moment.

Another step toward understanding the prosthetic nature of genes is understanding the defining structures of genetics. From the most complex level (the functioning human, animal, or plant organism) to the most basic level (the biochemical level), there is a continuum. If we think of these levels as the extremes, we can understand the conceptual structure that leads from one to the other. At the basic level, the building blocks of DNA are four nucleotides—adenine (A), guanine (G), thymine (T), and cytosine (C). These amino acids are always paired—adenine with thymine, guanine with cytosine. The "code" of the DNA molecule that determines the manufacture of a specific protein is made by repetitions of these four amino acids in a long strand. Another strand that is made up of the matching pairs exists beside the strand in sequence. So a string of GATACA will have a coordinated strand next to it of CTATGT. These paired nucleotides will be held together by a weak bond that comes undone when the DNA molecule divides down the center of the double helix and then reforms into two virtually identical molecules. At various points along the DNA molecule are loci that we have called *genes*. In the same way that we divide up the spectrum and assign arbitrary names to wavelengths, so we divide up the DNA molecule. But the division of sequences of nucleotides is somewhat arbitrary, as is the majority of DNA, which used to be called "junk." As weeds are plants that we don't use, so junk DNA can be DNA whose purpose, if any, is currently unknown, in that it appears not to produce a specific protein. Likewise a gene can be made up of several groupings of nucleotides (called *alleles*) in very separate and diverse locations. On the next level of complexity from DNA, chromosomes are made up of bundles of DNA strands that can be seen by microscope within the nucleus of the cell. Because these can be stained and seen, chromosomes are not so obviously "prosthetic," although in popular imagination and vision the dramatic visualized division of the cell, with the chromosomes performing their snake dance of duplication, takes on an aura of genes by proxy. When we talk about the double helix and genes, most people probably visualize the choreography of cell division with the stunning optical view of chromosomes reproducing in a kind of visible/invisible primal scene.

I have said that the gene is the locus on the DNA molecule that codes for a specific protein. If you imagine the double strand of DNA involving hundreds of thousands of base pairs of nucleotides, the question is, "Where is the gene?" In a human being, there are 3.2 million nucleotides. Based on the number of proteins in the human body, it has been estimated that one hundred thousand genes would be necessary to produce that variety of proteins. At a functional level, it is possible to experiment, removing a sequence of base pairs and then seeing what protein is or is not manufactured. The sequencing of the human genome revealed only about thirty thousand genes in the human genome, creating a bit of a puzzle about the efficacy of the model that was devised by Watson and Crick. Now the number appears to be closer to twenty-seven thousand.

The neat way that genetics is laid out in textbooks (and that I attempted to relate) has now undergone major revision. Instead of genes, scientists are now talking about "gene expression"—that is, the process by which coded information gets translated into cellular matter and structure. Epigenetics is the study of the way genes can be influenced and even changed by nongenetic factors. Gene expression and epigenetics are to genetics what Einstein's constant is to physics: they help create a seeming order in a very complex and shifting reality.

The point I am trying to make is that the gene, as such, is an amputated location, a place that is not there. In talking about genes and "junk" in the genome, scientists were dividing up what they thought of as functional sequences of nucleotides from the seemingly random distribution of nucleotides that are just "there." The trick is how to divide up the 3.2 billion nucleotides that are endless repetitions of four nucleotides—GATC. The most common metaphor concerning the human genome, which is defined as the total of all genes and junk in human DNA, is that the genome is "the book of life." By that metaphor, the letters GATC are the basic units of the book, corresponding to letters, and the letters GATC spell out sentences that are essentially genes. But the book of life is less like a book and more like a large and very messy hard drive with disruptions, gaps, spaces, and seemingly meaningless bits of information mixed up with very meaningful bits of information. If there is a book of life, its cover is the human body, and its contents are a kind of endless babble with some sense made every now and then. The body creates the illusion of a kind of prosthetic wholeness, the neat, seamless exterior held up like a *Playboy* pinup, while the fragmented and mysterious, even obscene, interior is no longer the blood and the guts but the impenetrable darkness, as Conrad might describe it, of the mysterious incantation of TACGATACTGG and so on into the abyss. The heart of darkness of being human is not the cannibalistic, sexualized moment suggested by Joseph Conrad's Marlow, but the monotonous voice of HAL in *2001:A Space Odyssey*, reciting word salad into infinity. Plucked from that racket is the prosthetic, the addition in grammar and language, the strand that can "read" as the place where the protein is made. This prosthetic, the gene, both dominates and subordinates our sense of the body—its contours and lineaments. It rationalizes some darker matrix that is still securely unknown to us despite our efflorescing technology. The gene is a substitute for the confusion of biochemical processes still unknown.

Genetics is a new way of examining old problems. In this sense, genetics represents a breakthrough, as did the discovery of the atom, the molecule, and subcellular chemistry. But each of these areas of study, while yielding results, opened many questions that could not be answered. After all, a frontier means both an opening of something new and a boundary beyond which we have not yet gone. We have no reason to believe that the conclusions we have drawn at this early stage of examination will hold or even that genetics will actually prove to the hopeful area that we are assuming it will be. Therefore, when we say *gene* or *genetics*, the word substitutes a hopeful sense of breakthrough for what also might be thought of as a bewildering confusion of information. We have learned that we can "read" DNA rather than see it as a babble of *lingua gataca*.

On a level of hypersignification, the genetic now becomes, anew, the racial. The primary reason given for the Human Genome Project and all genetic research is the promise of cures for genetic diseases and the development of genetic-specific drugs geared to particular human variations. Both of these reasons lead directly back to the genetics of race, since human populations, for all practical purposes, still tend to be seen as racial groups. Take for example a *New York Times* article reporting that "scientists studying the DNA of 52 human groups from around the world have concluded that people belong to five principal groups corresponding to the major geographical regions of the world: Africa, Europe, Asia, Melanesia, and the Americas. . . . These regions broadly correspond with popular notions of race."[3] The same researchers attempting to locate genetic similarities in racial groups find their work used by researchers who are trying to find diseases linked to specific groups. The litany is familiar—sickle-cell-anemia for blacks, Tay-Sachs and breast cancer for Jews, thalassemia for southern Europeans. Another *New York Times* story emphasized that Jews carry ten genetic diseases.[4] Compare this current assessment of Jews with the nineteenth-century eugenicist evaluations that saw Jews as particularly prone to diseases like epilepsy, neurasthenia, hysteria, mental illness, and so on.[5] There are not uncoincidentally few specifically "white" or "European" diseases: those are called "chronic" or just thought of as universal.

With this arrangement, to be the norm is to be "human"; to be ethnic or racial is to have diseases that require prosthetics at a genetic level. Rather than saying, as did nineteenth-century eugenicists, that various racial groups are inferior, defective, or degenerate, we can now say that various "populations" have "defective" genes that create birth "defects." The one-armed man or the eyeless woman in need of prosthetics now becomes the person born with a missing or erroneous allele or protein. The prosthetic level has become interior, intracellular, a grammatical mistake hidden within the *lingua gataca* that can be corrected by a supplementary addition. Of course this lack is no longer a permanent defect that can never be corrected. While now invisible, even without specific effects, the innermost notation of defect—that written in *lingua gataca* only readable by experts with complex machines of analysis—can be remediated, hypothetically in some imagined future, with an addition or correction on a genetic level. These invisible prosthetic additions will never be perceived visibly and so reside as transcriptions, rewrites no one will ever read.

We have to ask whether we will be creating a prosthetic space in genetics as we did over the mechanical replacement of body parts in the nineteenth century. For the nineteenth century, this space was defined by a kind of anaclitic confusion. Is the stump the missing limb, the tree, or the prosthetic? The prosthetic limb creates a kind of anxiety in personal space and stands in for the void that it is supposed to fill. The question of armlessness now becomes metonymically connected to the problem of the artificial limb that is trying to erase the void and so becomes the new void. The primitive horror of looking at the severed limb shaded into the visual horror of looking at the "lifelike" wooden limb. Likewise, the group of people with the genetic "defect" now become writ large as the problem of replacement or drug-prosthetic therapy. Rather than being "cured" by genetic therapy (which has not proven even partially successful at this point), the human population with the genetic "defect" becomes racialized anew as that group known to be "missing" the proper gene for hemoglobin production, in sickle-cell anemia, or for membrane permeability, in cystic fibrosis.

Likewise, people with genetic deafness are being seen as an "error" of coding and thus excluded from existence by prenatal screening or rendered "normal" through cochlear implants. The latter, because current policy requires parents to deliberately exclude sign language from their child's repertoire, also involves elimination of the main language of the Deaf. In a sense, sign language has been seen as a prosthesis for "normal speech"—a prosthesis that, like the stump or wooden leg, is now seen as old-fashioned and in need itself of replacement. What we have here is a cascading series of replacements reminiscent of Derrida's ideas of deferral or deferring—one replacement replacing another.

This transgressive existence of the genetic "defect" as the mistake that is correctable becomes even more problematic when we consider the way that genetic therapy works: a virus is emptied of its genetic matter, and the "right" genetic material is inserted into it. The virus is then injected into a human or an animal, and its mechanism allows the cells to be invaded and their genetic material altered. This sci-fi scenario, which has not thus far proved successful and has killed several people in the process of experimentation, carries a weighty signification. The defective race must be infected, invaded, and altered by a disease to correct a disease. Thus the invisibility of the prosthesis becomes linked to an invasion/contamination scenario that we have seen before in countless sci-fi films—perhaps most notably Ridley Scott's *Alien*. This "cure" scenario also repeats on some fundamental level the racial-purity fears of a hundred years earlier, in which defective races were seen as "infecting" the purity of more advance races. Now the infection scenario is reversed as the advanced races deliberately infect the defective races to correct their defects.

Further, the visual isolation and stigmatization of the wearer of the prosthetic limb now becomes the institutionalized visualization of the group under the lens of genetic scanning. Populations that are overresearched will tend to be those in which more genetic anomalies are found. In other words, the group "white" tends not to be studied as a social group, while the groups "African American," "Hispanic," and "Jewish" tend to be studied. In that case, it is no surprise that genetic differences will be found. Thus, scrutiny will produce observations that will produce corrections. In this scenario, prosthesis is more about the observation than the conclusion. We can speak of prosthetic process within a space of prosthesis.

In addition to specific groups entering into a prosthetic relation to a dominant group, a new development is well under way. Drugs that are tailored to specific ethnic or racial groups are being developed. There is a genetic component to this work since the notion is that certain populations will have diseases specific to those groups, probably because of hypothetical genetic differences. As we have indicated, the genetic cause will replace a far more likely complex of social causes and political consequences as individuals and races get blamed and exploited for "their" diseases. Indeed, several companies in the United States, including Alcon Laboratories, have already created pharmaceuticals that are tailored for African Americans: Travatan is marketed as "the first glaucoma drug to demonstrate greater effectiveness in black patients,"[6] and BiDil, a cardiac medication made by NitroMed, has been approved by the US Food and Drug Administration (FDA) as "the first heart failure medication specifically for African American patients."[7]

The drug BiDil provides an excellent case in point. Jonathan D. Kahn has traced the history of this drug and shown how racializing medicine and using genetic explanations for medical conditions lead to bad science and abuse of the drug industry for profit.[8] This drug, which is a combination of two previously available generic drugs, failed on its first round through the FDA because of poor testing and design and bad statistical work. But with statistical rearrangement of the initial test, NitroMed has been permitted to design and test using only black patients. The new application was based on a few articles, some written by the patent applicants themselves, that claim that blacks die from heart failure at a rate that is twice that of whites. Kahn shows that this statistic was used and published widely in scientific and medical journals, as well as in the public press, even though it is completely false. According to Kahn, the more accurate statistic, based on more recent numbers, is that the mortality-rate difference between whites and blacks is virtually nil.[9] Kahn concludes that, even without hard evidence, researchers will grab at the genetic racial explanation because it is easier to hypothesize an individual biological cause than to pay attention to the complexities of social, economic, and cultural factors. Race may factor in as racism rather than genetics, according to a report from the Institute of Medicine of the National Academies, which found that racial and ethnic minorities tend to receive lower-quality health care than whites, even when researchers correct for income, age, and insurance status.[10] Another study indicates that people who perceive themselves as the objects of racism will have higher blood pressure.[11] The reality is that diseases, even if associated with genetic causes, will include a complex interaction between the genes and the environment. This Troy Duster refers to as "a complex interaction of social forces and biological feedback loops."[12]

Thus, with the advent of drugs that are tailored to racial groups, the prosthetic element is now doubled. What we get is eugenics squared: to be of a racialized group is to be in a prosthetic relation to the dominant group, as we have seen above. Now we add another element: to be of a racialized group requires additional therapies to cure that group of the diseases that are inherent to the group because it is racialized. So coursing through the bloodstream of all racialized groups will be the hidden prosthetic of drugs designed to make that group "human" and "normal." This is the truly biocultural moment in which humanity is redefined in terms of medical interventions to correct the "defect" of race. Thus, to be human is to be normalized, which means that one must have the prosthetic corrective that is purchased from globalized pharmaceutical corporations whose existence is based on achieving this widespread consumption. At its best, the prosthetic is no longer lifelike but becomes life itself, inserting itself into unseen biological processes. We are witnessing the ultimate moment of prosthetics, in which the differences among the tree stump, the limb stump, and the prosthetic stump dissolve. The genetic model combined with the advent of gene therapy, genopharmacology, and segmented marketing gives us a prosthetic that resides within the living being sharing the very life processes that all living things share. This opportunistic, in all senses of the word, occupation inaugurates the biotechnological existence in a step that makes the cyborg obsolete. We see layers and cascades of prosthetic hypersignification, from the prosthetic nature of the gene and DNA to the geneticizing of social categories like race and finally to the solution of the problem of race through biotechnological fixes inspired by the rapacity of global capitalism.

We can say that we are no longer stumped by genes, but we are more likely to find ourselves trumped by genes, particularly since this transition is happening at breakneck speed in the context of a largely uninformed public sphere. Although many of us are highly informed about the social and cultural issues that arise around race, we are in great need of a biocultural education that would allow us to confront the changes that are happening outside the public's ken and inside the corridors of hospitals, research institutions, and biotech firms. If we allow a prosthetic space to develop regarding the corporate and institutional takeover of the human genome and the genomes of various indigenous and racialized groups via patenting and copyright, we will see a relation of power and substitution continuing from the social to the genetic. In the prosthetic space, meanings and biotechnical objects are put in place of, added to, and created as a supplement to existing definitions of being human. The relationship that we are describing—the politics of prosthesis—cedes that meaning-giving power, the power to add something as a correction, to corporate, institutional, and even personal entities without discussing the process. In the biocultural space, however, the substitution becomes a reservoir of meaning—a helping limb, as it were—to explain and decode the mystery of the hidden substitution. The prosthetic describes the lack, and the biocultural suggests the meaning of the lack and the congealed power that becomes embodied in the prosthesis itself.

CHAPTER SIX

Diagnosis

A Biocultural Critique of Certainty

The social model of disability ultimately relies on the distinction between disability and impairment. That model has been very useful in defining the nature of oppression and the social construction of disability. One leg of the analysis, the impairment one, relies on a medical diagnosis to confirm the nature of the impairment. While medical diagnosis is the bedrock of any attempt to understand disease, it is not without its problems. In this chapter, I want to raise some questions about the ontological status of diagnosis and by extension ideas of certainty. I'm not doing this to question whether it is possible to diagnose, nor am I questioning the often helpful and therapeutic outcome of diagnoses. What I am wondering about is the aura of faith that accompanies the process of diagnosis. I am also well aware that medical practitioners, particularly those in psychiatry and psychology, are cognizant that diagnoses can be approximate and multiple. It is also true that in the United States and elsewhere diagnosis is required in order to receive insurance reimbursements. Nevertheless, there is a patina, in popular culture and even medical culture, in which diagnosis is taken as the first principle in treatment, outcome assessment, and research in general.

In this essay I want to concentrate less on general medicine and more on psychiatry, where I think the problem of diagnosis is particularly vexed. One could argue that in the scenario of a patient with a broken leg or with cholera, there would be no special interest in the social-cultural surround of the patient. The diagnosis would be unproblematic and the treatment obvious. Of course, no diagnosis is actually unproblematic or freed from social and cultural issues. Anne Fausto-Sterling has shown us that even bone-density diagnosis is dependent on social and cultural factors.[1] So when we discuss psychiatric diagnoses, we have to be especially careful to pay attention to such factors. In the case of psychiatric disorders, particularly affective disorders, there is a complex cultural and historical scenario, I will argue, that has in effect formed and preselected the categories available for diagnosis, positioned the diagnostician and the patient within an inevitable power relation, and raised basic problems around the activity of diagnosis itself. As treatment is dependent on these diagnoses and on the production of both disease and cure, how ethical can an approach to "bio" be? In addition, I raise the question of how there can be an ethics of a disease entity whose existence is far from certain.[2]

In pursuing this point, I want to focus particularly on obsessive-compulsive disorder (OCD). If we begin with the *Diagnostic and Statistical Manual of Mental Disorders* (known as *DSM IV TR*)[3] classification of OCD, we will be able to interrogate notions of being "mentally ill" implied in a bioethical approach.[4] The *DSM IV TR* is used by practitioners to arrive at a numerical code for diagnostic and insurance-reimbursement purposes (for example, the code for OCD is 300.3). The manual appears to be definitive and is written in a style that indicates authority and lack of doubt—this despite the fact that there is considerable play within and between diagnoses (made less of a problem by the inclusion of the idea of "comorbidity"—which emphasizes that many other symptoms might be present beyond those grouped into the diagnosis).[5] Many people have written about the problems inherent in the *DSM*, and I can't go into those in this chapter. But I want to pinpoint that, by its own admission, the *DSM* was designed to "improve communication" among practitioners.[6] Thus it is less of a bible and more of a playbook. What appears in it is more tentative than might first appear to be the case. The epistemological and ontological category of a particular diagnosis rests on its derivation from the *DSM*, but the *DSM* cannot itself provide anything resembling certainty, although it aspires to certainty.[7]

One might want to begin by saying that the clinical entity of OCD is far from an established and naturally occurring phenomenon. It may be true that humans have always counted, ordered, checked, washed, collected, and so on. And it may be true that the human mind can have a tendency to return repeatedly and continually to some thought or mental activity. However, when we group a set of mental or physical behaviors into a disease entity, we take a step that is constitutive but also imaginary and symbolic.[8] Having created this category that makes "sense" of random or seemingly linked behaviors, we can then assign people and their behaviors to those categories.

Diagnosis is a complex process in which a person's behaviors and thoughts, capable of being seen in many registers, are transmuted into the specific register of symptoms. That transmutation is part of a continuous process in which the observer places the subject into a category of what might be called the "prediagnosed" or "diagnosable." Of course we are all potentially prediagnosed, but in reality we only slide into that category when, in some liminal moment, we move or are moved from person to patient. Likewise, the observer must shift in that register from fellow human, coconversationalist, to diagnostician. A diagnostician is no longer engaging in a "natural" and equal exchange with the interlocutor. Rather, the diagnostician must move from personal, moral, and social judgments made in the course of the haphazard but explicable space of conversation to the seemingly more stratified, scientific, and regulated kind of description that is found in the *DSM*. From one perspective we may say that this shift is one that defamiliarizes one modality of being by making another estranged form of interacting seem more natural. Apparently normal conversation, then, becomes in fact an occasion for symptom gathering on the part of the practitioner, and normal thinking becomes transformed into clinical analysis.

How strange this is might be illustrated by an amusing "report" from the satiric newspaper the *Onion* from March 23, 2009. In a story with the headline, "98% of Babies Manic Depressive," the paper goes on to report:

> A new study published in *The Journal Of Pediatric Medicine* found that a shocking 98% of all infants suffer from bipolar disorder. "The majority of our subjects, regardless of size, sex, or race, exhibited extreme mood swings, often crying one minute and then giggling playfully the next," the study's author Dr. Steven Gregory told reporters. "Additionally we found that most babies had trouble concentrating during the day, often struggled to sleep at night, and could not be counted on to take care of themselves—all classic symptoms of manic depression." Gregory added that nearly 100% of infants appear to suffer from the poor motor skills and impaired speech associated with Parkinson's disease.[9]

The humor of this piece is dependent on the fact that we don't generally use the diagnostic register to talk about the behavior of very young infants (although there are feeding and eating disorders listed in the *DSM* for infants). But why should we use that register at all? Clearly there are reasons to think diagnostically in categorical ways, but what are the foundations for such thinking about thinking diagnostically? Is diagnosis the only way of knowing, shaping, and collecting these behaviors into putatively clear and distinct entities? Does the "correct" diagnosis then produce a specific and beneficial cure?[10]

The *DSM* is itself an Enlightenment project of the first order. Its goal is to categorize and "know" the discrete entities of mental illness that it tautologically predicts will exist. The process by which these categories arise has been very haphazard and arbitrary: literally the result of committee work done by small groups of practitioners, influenced by social and economic forces, and the result of voting and consensus. The fact that the disorders change over time and that new symptoms and groupings arise in each edition of the *DSM* only emphasizes the contingent nature of diagnosis. Tellingly, in the seven years between the last and the current editions of the *DSM*, the number of categories and subcategories increased from 297 to 374, amounting to almost 25 percent, or about ten new disorders or diseases per year. The newest edition of the *DSM* will probably follow along in this exponential increase of diagnostic categories.

The implication of the word *diagnosis* is that we can know a disease apart from other diseases or apart from anything. *Dia* means both "through" or "thoroughly." Those rather different meanings point to a profound ambivalence in the concept of diagnosis. If you gain knowledge "through" something, is the knowledge gained *of* the subject or the object? If the object is the means through which you know, then is the knowledge of the subject or the object? What makes the knowledge "thorough" in that case? *Gnosis*, as knowledge, implies the certainty of religious knowledge, and its adjective, *gnostic*, is opposed to the doubtful—that is to say, full of doubt— knowledge of the agnostic. The heyday of the use of *gnosis* and of *diagnosis* in the English language was the second half of the nineteenth century, coinciding with the rise of evangelical Christianity, as well as the professionalization of medicine. Without making too much of this point, could we not see the physician as displacing the divine as the source for certain knowledge? Diagnosis in this scenario would be the medical equivalent of the theological certainty offered by a knowing—in this case a knowing of the body if not the soul.

Understanding Diagnosis as a New Kind of Certain Knowing

Knowing someone diagnostically may seem to present the most certain kind of knowing among a variety of knowings, but I would argue that in fact it represents a serious type of Lacanian misrecognition, that is, a knowing based on not knowing. We might explore this misrecognition by starting with the first stage of diagnosis—the symptom. This stage begins with a presentation of a symptom or group of symptoms to the practitioner. But even this beginning has a prehistory, since the patient has to know that he or she "has" a symptom. To "know" one "has" a symptom initiates the cascading effect of misrecognition or what we might consider the earliest phase of the diagnostic mirror phase. First, you must sense something within the self, fit it into a taxonomy, use a preexisting language of description, and communicate that "something" to a practitioner. Each one of those steps will therefore involve intuitions, conformity to norms and standards, rendering the physical or psychic intelligible through the deformations of language, and shaping that response to the listening practitioner. In this sense there are no "natural" or "inherent" symptoms apart from those communal and social ways of knowing the body and categorizing what is sensed or not sensed as symptoms. For example, to sense a symptom can be particularly complex when the symptom itself involves not a presence, but an absence of feeling or well-being. Anhedonia, for example, is the state of not feeling pleasure. Hypoactive sexual desire disorder (HSDD) concerns a lack or absence of sexual fantasies and desire for sexual activity for some period. Even stranger, situational HSDD is lack of desire for one's current partner. Such a nonfeeling will only become apparent in a group that stresses the importance of feeling pleasure or the discursive requirements of sexuality in particular relationships and settings. It would seem that something like pain would be less dependent on the social and situational. However, David Morris points out the very biocultural aspect of pain, which seems at face value to be a natural and immanent sensation unmediated by culture or language.[11] Morris notes that pain "is decisively shaped or modified by individual human minds and specific human cultures."[12] And of course, psychic pain is even more dependent on discursive knowledges.

To sense a symptom, then, is to become involved in a matrix of significations whose meanings are more or less purely social and culture. What happens when we move from sensing to presenting? Indeed, presenting symptoms is a phenomenal part of sociability, as we routinely ask upon seeing one another, "How are you?" We are hailed into the language of medicine in a neomedicalized Gramscian sense each time we meet another and engage in phatic conversation. We are required to report on our mental and physical well-being or absence of well-being. Symptom presentation is part of the performance of everyday life, the collective understanding of bodies, and thus the advice given by the other is part of that sociability.

But what happens when the other is a professional diagnostician?

The conversation ends then, and clinic hours begin. The shift from sociability to medical interaction changes the agency involved. One's "having" a symptom is now made less active.[13] One becomes a function of one's symptom, and the symptom becomes a sign in a text to be deciphered (and deciphered quickly, given the pressures of time and money in today's medical practice). Any notion of agency on the part of the symptom presenter is transformed to docility, in Foucault's sense, and the agency is transferred, seemingly, to the diagnostician, whose job is now a kind of detective work. But even the diagnostician's agency is only apparent, given that the list of possible interpretations is predetermined by the *DSM* in this case or by professional guidelines in general. Thus we might speculate that the diagnostician becomes less of a bricoleur, cobbling things together from a range of possibilities, and more of a factory worker sorting nuts and bolts into their proper boxes. Of course, each instance will have its own parameters, and no doubt there are excellent detectives out there as well as skilled sorters.

Seeing the diagnostician as someone engaged in deciphering a riddle raises the cultural specter of Oedipus before the Sphinx. In that story, a pile of bones lay in a crevasse below the Sphinx, the remains of those unsuccessful in answering the question, "What walks on four legs in the morning, two at midday, and three at night?" The question is in fact a medical question, one that traces the ability of the body to ambulate or not at various points in physical development. In some sense, the Sphinx is asking of the human race, "How are you?" Oedipus, whose name itself relates to the ability to walk properly—"swollen foot"—is a symptom bearer for the human race, and he evidently must walk with some degree of limp in order to bear his name. In answering the Sphinx, he is able to diagnose the physical problem because he himself perhaps knows something about the complexity of ambulating.[14] His actions of killing his father and marrying his mother then cause the state to fall ill with the symptom of infertility. This time Oedipus will diagnose and cure the city, but his own lack of knowing will prevent him from finding the correct diagnosis until he realizes that he is the *pharmakon*—both cause and cure, according to Derrida—and must be driven out in order to make the city well again.

In what I'm seeing as an Oedipal version of diagnosis, the modern practitioner attempts to answer the riddle presented by the patient's symptom. The bodies in the pile are those who have been misdiagnosed, who have asked themselves the wrong question or presented the wrong symptoms. The diagnostician never falls into the crevasse, but rather the risk resides with the reporting subject. Yet we could also see the diagnostician as answering the riddle only at the point where he or she misrecognizes the complicity within himself or herself. As with Oedipus, it is the lack of "gnosis" within the "diagnostic" that triggers the cascade of tragic events. The diagnostician knows "through" the patient, but in *knowing through* he or she leaves out the *knowing of* the categorical ontogeny of the knowing. In the biocultural scenario I am presenting, the lack of knowing of one's history, the history of not only the symptom but the disease entity, as with Oedipus, can produce the outcome of a successful diagnosis that fails to cure because it is successful in one sense of knowing only.

To know and diagnose in our current world is to know and select something from a list of many other things. As mentioned, it is a decipherment through sorting rather than analysis. To diagnose is to attempt to emphasize difference. The act of setting OCD apart from other anxiety disorders, for example, will always be difficult if not impossible since the setting apart denies the clinal nature of experience and sensation. To set behaviors and mental actions apart in diagnosis (as opposed to "analysis," which looks at a totality and breaks it apart) is in effect done in an imaginary space only, since if there is a real space—in this biocultural sense I am proposing—it will always be a clinal one. The paradox is that the definitive act of diagnosis of mental disorders will almost always produce comorbid states because no anxiety disorder exists alone.

The idea of comorbidity is, in effect, a tacit admission that diagnostics are always imprecise, overlapping other disease states, blurred at the borders. The clinal, in which there is an infinite range of change within a continuum, should be opposed to the diagnostic, in which the correct outcome can only be one (or more) fixed location(s). However, the cline's incline, according to the derivation of the word from the Greek for "slope," may provide more certainty than the level-headed fixed point of diagnosis, which—by denying the askew nature of gnosis—becomes a slippery slope itself.

Wittgenstein notes the problem inherent in any diagnostic act of certainty: "I know there is a sick man lying here? Nonsense! I am sitting at his bedside. I am looking attentively into his face—So I don't know there is a sick man lying here? Neither the question nor the assertion makes sense."[15] Neither statement makes sense because the act of being certain is itself a kind of language game. Wittgenstein explores the idea of certainty and notes: "Certainty is *as it were* a tone of voice in which one declares how things are, but one does not infer from the tone of voice that one is justified."[16] The *DSM* aids clinicians in achieving this tone of voice—what might be called authority—by providing categorical imperatives (not in the Kantian sense).

How Discrete is the Object?

I have argued in *Obsession: A History* that OCD is not a discrete clinical entity.[17] I make that point in several ways. First, I provide a genealogy of obsession to show that it has a taproot in culture, society, and history. I trace the development of a growing interest in obsession from the eighteenth through the nineteenth centuries in the UK, in the United States, and on the Continent. What becomes obvious in that genealogy is that certain groups of symptoms, which we now assemble into OCD, were assembled differently in the past. The gradual grouping of those symptoms into entities like monomania and idée fixe coincided with a larger cultural interest in obsessive behavior and thought and with obsession as a regnant cultural paradigm. On the one hand, obsession becomes a kind of cultural goal focused on the idea of increasing human productivity through the single-minded application of the self to the environment; on the other hand, it becomes pathological. In the former category we find the rise of the professions and of the modern university, in which specialization, continuous work, and obsessive focus become hallmark traits. Interestingly, the rise of psychiatry and neurology was also conditioned on the obsessive study of obsessives and hysterics. Linked to this line of thinking is the development of the cult of the genius, who is defined as a person whose intellectual or artistic abilities come yoked to the ills or harms of the single-minded pursuit of a practice. The nervous breakdown then becomes an expected and understandable event in the autobiography or narrative portrayal of the genius—and the cause of the breakdown is attributed to working too hard, doing one thing too much. Thus the cause and the symptom are the same.

Meanwhile, the pathological side is seen, in addition to the nervous breakdown, in the rise of disease entities like neurasthenia, the disease of modernity that is influenced by excessive work and concentration. Indeed, the rise of psychology, psychiatry, and neurology is based to a great degree on the studying of people with such monomanias. Books like Richard von Krafft-Ebing's *Psychopathia Sexualis* is nothing but an obsessive compendium of hundreds of sexual obsessions. The hand-in-glove relationship between diagnosis and disease is seen clearly in books such as this, which assemble random sexual behaviors into disease entities, which then proliferate such diseases through the agency of diagnosis and publication. Pathology then becomes a function of diagnosis, which itself is a function of pathology. We might call this the diagnostic circle, a tautological process that produces a reductive inevitability. To diagnose is to define; to define is to diagnose. Definitions produce diagnoses, which in turn produce definitions.

Without going into great detail, it is possible to say that the *DSM* diagnosis of OCD is conditioned on creating a firewall between the larger cultural practices and the appearance in an individual of some of those practices. The Enlightenment subject lives and breathes in the psychiatric or therapeutic patient because frequently only the simplest notions of identity are permitted. Any suggestion that there is a codependency between person and culture goes against the idea that the truly well person must be independent, just as the disabled person who needs a personal assistant is seen as a failure of personhood as defined by the same notions. It is certainly true that the work of Stephen Mitchell, Lewis Aron, and Neil Altman and other relational psychoanalysts emphasizes "a balance between internal and external relationships, real and imagined, the intrapsychic and the interpersonal, the intrasubjective, the individual and the social."[18]

Diagnosis is always synchronic. It always takes place in a clinical present moment of certainty. It has to willfully suppress the diachronicity of its own coming into being, because such history might reveal contingency, chance, convention, and so on. By definition, the diagnostic criteria of the moment are always right, and previous criteria are almost always wrong. In that sense, according to the synchronic perspective, the history of medicine is a history, largely, of error. Through trial and error, so the argument goes, what was wrong in the past is discovered and discarded. The new criteria are based on corrections of the old mistakes. Thus the current diagnostic criteria are always the last step, the hopeful, utopian moment, the final correction of a history of error. In this sense, the diagnostic process is amnesiac and is constitutionally incapable of being uncertain about its certainty. The only thing the amnesiac knows for certain is that he or she is here in the moment. The next phase of the amnesia will come when the current criteria are updated or discarded. Then it will be impossible to remember the former correctness of that last stage of diagnosis, and that discarded diagnostic category will fall into the crevasse of error. As with the Oedipal nature of diagnosis, the pile of bodies below the Sphinx is the wreckage of discarded diagnostic entities.

In suggesting, as I have, that OCD has a history, then, I presume to indicate the genealogy of the category of OCD; connect the current diagnosis with cultural, historical, and political practice; and show how simply producing this diagnosis now is somewhat problematic. I am suggesting that the past is not a pile of bones, no longer vital, but the story told, the archeology of the narrative of how those bones met their fate. In the case of OCD, if we can see the transformations, disjunctions, and paradigms that have changed over time, we can better see the contingent, aleatory, and liminal nature of the contemporary diagnosis. If that is the case, then the simple rules that govern a diagnosis of impairment must be put into doubt.

One might want to suggest that the encounter between patient and practitioner is one dependent on history and yet at the same time is a singular encounter. To be ethical in the broadest sense of the term, the encounter must constitute a dialectic between those conditions, must be based on mutually involved subjects interacting with each other in a time-space continuum. As Lewis Aron notes, "When I say that psychoanalysis is a mutual endeavor, I mean, more precisely, that the patient and the analyst create a unique system in which . . . there is a reciprocal influence and mutual regulation."[19] The validity of the moment of that interaction must take into account the "nowness" of the moment, the uniqueness of the encounter through the uniqueness of both patient and practitioner. The patient brings experience, and the practitioner brings knowledge of the diagnostic criteria and treatment options. But with psychiatric encounters, particularly, this asymmetrical mutuality is often subsumed to the demands of time, institutional requirements, and professional practices. The encounter must take place in the consciousness of time, but time in the sense of the *longue durée*. Indeed, the historical continuum is suppressed in the interest of making the diagnostic criteria less contingent and in some major sense developmental. Thus the diagnostic criteria can only become inscribed as a kind of law or writ if they are presented as having no ontological basis. No one claims a law is invalid because of the existence of previous laws; however, current diagnoses might have less sovereignty if the existence of previous diagnostic criteria were more apparent. One might ask the question, why is hysteria a less valid diagnosis than mania? Why have we largely abandoned one and kept the other?[20]

In effect, the diagnostician has to balance the singular moment of encounter with the customary nomenclature and categories provided by the profession. His or her diagnosis will amount to a decision or judgment based on the current moment and the current criteria. But the criteria will be simultaneously ahistorical in their claim to universality and deeply historical in their coming into being. Diagnosis will require a repression of that coming into being in favor of the moment of judgment. Thus there will be a suppressed conflict between custom and justice.

Such a conflict takes us back to the tragic theme in diagnosis, now requiring that we turn from Oedipus to his daughter Antigone. If Oedipus is the diagnostician, Antigone is the patient. A long critical tradition has tried to diagnose her and her motives. Why does she willingly give up her life in order to bury her brother? Who is guilty? Creon or Antigone? Sophocles's play is one that continually cries out for defining diagnostics. Kant, Hegel, Lacan, and Zizek, among others, have seen the main character as representing some fundamental ethical position. Antigone's conflict between *dike*, or justice, and *nomos*, or the customary laws, is highlighted in the play by Creon's insistence on the priority of state law while Antigone appeals to the authority of custom in the proper burial of her brother. This is, in fact, the conflict facing the diagnostician. Is a diagnostician involved in a just decision or a customary one? Is the decision an ethical one or a political one? Is there a gap between those binaries? Lacan argues that Antigone's act represents a pure act because it defies the Symbolic order and is contrary to the pleasure principle in its rush toward death. Zizek goes further and sees Antigone as the focus of ethico-political debate because her act is both in defiance of the Symbolic order and at the same time dependent on it.[21] In either case, Antigone is seen as an exemplary figure, and from the point of view of diagnosis, her state of indeterminacy demands a judgment from the viewers of this play, who need to give her a label, to name her condition. That requirement inevitably falls into whether we consider the dictate of Creon a singular act of his own diagnostic criteria, a law unto itself, or whether Antigone's reference to custom and history has greater sway. In terms of the problematic of diagnosis we have been considering, we might ask whether the cumulative history of psychiatry, ignored and upheld in the singular act of diagnosing a patient, is more important than the individual relation between the patient and the practitioner.

We might then see the problem of diagnosis to be a problem in some sense between ethics and politics. Simon Critchley says of Derrida's ideas:

> On the one hand ethics is left defined as the infinite responsibility of unconditional hospitality. Whilst, on the other hand the political can be defined as the taking of a decision without any determinate transcendental guarantees. Thus the hiatus in Levinas allows Derrida both to affirm the primacy of an ethics of hospitality, whilst leaving open the sphere of the political as a realm of risk and danger.[22]

To this point, Zizek comments, in the context of his discussion of Antigone, "the ethical is thus the (back)ground of undecidability, while the political is the domain of decision(s)."[23] We can then say that diagnosis hesitates before the undecidability between *nomos* and *dike*, between custom and justice. In that sense, it contains within it the Aristotelian definition of tragedy—involving the choice the protagonist must make between two impossible courses based on a kind of knowledge that is itself a kind of blindness involving both awareness and lack of awareness.

At the same time there is an undecidable opposition between a concept of hospitality, which implies a guest-host relationship that is easily reversible so that host can become guest and vice versa, and the political decision, in which the sovereign can never change places with the governed except through the most violent of means. Is the physician a fellow interlocutor or a grand inquisitor? In the world of bioethics, as it stands, the patient has rights but never the right to be the physician. (And if the patient happens to be a physician, then that professional title must disappear in the move to patienthood.) Thus, the rule of hospitality is barred, and the state of exception rules.

One of the means by which the sovereignty of the practitioner holds sway is through the metaphorics and metonymics of diagnostic representation. Hospitality requires an undecidability, but diagnosis in its political sense requires decision. Like all sovereign decisions, it requires the certainty that comes from the amnesis of past and the dissolution of commensurability between subject and object. In that moment we have described, the ethics of bioethics become useless, and the biopower of the instant becomes the law of the realm. Through a thorough understanding of the diagnostic moment, we can become aware of the tragedy of certainty.

Indeed, bioethics' key concepts might not map so easily onto a framework that includes biopower and biocultural imperatives, including a profound sense of historicity and of social construction. Concepts like autonomy, beneficence, and nonmalfeasance require a dully positivist mentality to work or be considered sufficient. And justice, as it is considered in bioethics, needs to be put into dialogue with custom, as it is in Greek tragedy. In the case of psychiatric disorders, how would a biocultural model of diagnosis work? Greek tragedy offers us a medical model of sorts. Aristotle's idea of catharsis is taken directly from Greek medical knowledge. A cathartic is a powerful purgative administered to clear the bowels. Aristotle's notion is that the audience's pity and fear, in reaction to the fate of the protagonist, would purge them of their emotions and leave them feeling cleansed and emptied. In other words, for Aristotle, the cure offered to characters within the play, the cure administered by fate and by the gods, as well as by the narrative process, would be heuristic and salutory.

We might then say that something in the diagnostic process might in fact provide a curative modality. If that were the case, what would that curative modality look like? As we said, the diagnosis would have to be attained in a condition of mutuality, one that took into consideration the history of not only the patient and the practitioner but also the profession itself. Pity and fear might be the motivating factors in that mutuality: each side of the diagnostic equation would both fear for the outcome and pity various fates of the other. In the permutations involved in that complex process, the practitioner would be conscious of the self-otherness of the patient, placing himself or herself in the futurity of diagnostic process (for who will be immune from being diagnosed?) and, at the same time, fear both the incorrect diagnosis and probably the correct one as well. So when Tiresias says to Oedipus, "You do not know who you are!" that caution must apply to both the patient and the practitioner. As the theater of Greek tragedy provides a location to explore that question, the space of diagnosis must also be aware of its theatricality and provide a place to pose, if not answer, that central question. Bioethics, too, must expand its work to be a chorus to that central drama and can only do so if it understands fully the implications of a more profound complexity than it has heretofore allowed itself to engage. And finally, disability will have to be reconsidered as both part of the diagnosis and part of the diagnosing. Oedipus's limp and Philoctetes's wound are both diagnosable impairments and impairments that confer an ability to diagnose.

CHAPTER SEVEN

A Disability Studies Case for Physician-Assisted Suicide

There has been a curious, in my mind, linkage between disability identity and the fraught area of physician-assisted suicide (PAS). In some circles of disability activism it has become a truism that you can't be for disability and for PAS along with euthanasia.[1] There is a strong pressure in our field to toe the line on this issue and to see any attempt to make distinctions between PAS and euthanasia as part of a "slippery slope" argument. However, I believe it is very possible to be for assisted suicide while maintaining a disability identity. This essay will attempt to make that case.

In speaking for PAS, I want to make the obvious point that I am not opposing disability studies or its tenets. Rather I am advocating disability studies in the fullest sense. I would hope that the field is one that encourages discussion and debate about all issues. And I welcome others to join me or to disagree with me.

I want to state my position clearly first. I am for PAS as defined by the laws now in force in Oregon and Washington (and would be glad to see at least one further safeguard included—a mandatory consultation with a disability advocate). My position aligns with that of Autonomy, the disability group in favor of PAS.[2] Under the Oregon law a state resident diagnosed with six months or less to live is allowed to ask, in writing, for a lethal drug—in this case a prescription for an overdose of barbiturates. The letter of request must be witnessed by two people, one of whom cannot benefit materially from the death. A doctor is not allowed to suggest or originate the idea of killing oneself to a patient. Two doctors must agree that the person has six months or less to live. They may recommend a consultation with a psychiatrist if necessary. There is a two-week waiting period, after which the person must be reminded that they can rescind their request. If the person still wishes to continue, the doctor sends a written prescription to a nonhospital pharmacist, and the person or a friend must retrieve the drugs from the pharmacist. Then the person can do whatever he or she wants with the drugs. The doctor is not required to be present at the suicide unless the person asks the doctor to be present. And the doctor cannot administer the drug.

As I said, I agree with this law, and I feel that it has built-in safeguards, but in future laws I would want legislators to include a consult with a disability advocate.

Many people use the terms *PAS* and *euthanasia* interchangeably, but a key point is that PAS is not euthanasia. Euthanasia is when a doctor kills a patient. Physician-assisted suicide is when a person kills him- or herself with drugs that can only be gotten legally with a prescription. A better name would be "self-administered, legal overdose." I am inherently a pacifist and against murder in all forms, with the usual qualifiers about self-defense and just wars, but I am for suicide under these conditions. Suicide is, by the way, legal in all the states of the United States. Physician-assisted suicide is currently only legal in the states of Oregon, Washington, and Montana, although similar laws have been proposed in California, New York, and other states. To me, Oregon's law seems a reasonable one that permits people to die with their families present in a relatively peaceful way. The current alternative to PAS is that a person would have to die by illegal means, with a family member, friend, or physician engaging in a criminal act. The methods now available in all non-PAS states involve a violent act like shooting oneself, placing a plastic bag over the head, crashing a car deliberately, turning on the gas jets, putting a hose from the exhaust into one's car, or jumping from a roof. None of these would permit a person to leave this world with family members and friends present, with candles, music, or whatever enhancements the dying person requests. And anyone who has ever had a dear one or relative kill themselves in one of these ways can testify how horrible it is to walk into a room and see that person with their brains blown out or laid out bloody and injured on a slab in the morgue.

So how did disability activists and scholars get in the position of opposing legislation that has as its aim a removing of medical power over a person (the power to withhold certain drugs)? Why should the mostly progressive disability community be lining up with the right-to-life movement, the American Medical Association, religious fundamentalists, and conservatives throughout the country, feeding that beast so that it will bite back with more and more favorable court decisions that will ultimately work toward the elimination of the right to privacy that governs the rights to abortion and sexual freedom, among others?

The issue is more pressing than the discomfort of associating with such diametrically opposed political groups. Disability activism and study has been based on certain principles. The idea that the medical and charity models of disability are destructive seems to suggest caution when the most powerful medical association in the world unites with very influential religious organizations. As if that were not enough, the fundamental question in the PAS movement involves two principles central to disability activism and scholarship—the right to live independently and the right to privacy. The first stresses the right of people with disabilities to have autonomy and control over their own bodies; the second ensures that medical records, medical decisions, and the right to control one's own body—including the right to abortion, contraception, and sexual orientation—are safeguarded.

An interesting window opens up when we look at the George W. Bush administration's failed attempt to quash the Oregon law. The legal case of *Gonzales v. Oregon* was based on the idea that since barbiturates are controlled substances, the federal government could intervene and say that the Oregon law, which relies on the use of such drugs, was illegal. The implication is that the federal government could prevent the use of legal marijuana and of course marijuana in general. At the time, a friend of the court brief was filed supporting the Bush administration's claim by Not Dead Yet; ADAPT; the Center on Disability Studies, Law and Human Policy at Syracuse University; the Center for Self-Determination; the Hospice Patients Alliance; the Mouth Magazine/Freedom Clearinghouse; the National Council on Independent Living; the National Spinal Cord Injury Association; Self-Advocates Becoming Empowered; TASH; and the World Institute on Disability.[3] Considering that the case was more generally about whether the federal government has the right to tell states what their citizens can and cannot do with their bodies, it is remarkable that so many disability organizations were willing to side with Attorney General Alberto Gonzales, who crafted the legal statements that allowed the open-ended war on terror, fired liberal federal attorneys, denied the right to habeas corpus, approved wire taps on US citizens, and the like. Invasion of privacy should be especially troubling to people with disabilities, who want their own medical records, genetic information, and so on kept from outside entities like insurance companies, potential employers, and the government itself.

A final point on the strange bedfellows issue. *Gonzales v. Oregon* was originally named *Ashcroft v. Oregon*. The Justice Department, under the leadership of then Attorney General John Ashcroft, chose to mount an attack on the Oregon law not out of sympathy with the disability issue, but because of Ashcroft's own right-to-life, conservative agenda. In fact, the Supreme Court had already ruled in *Washington v. Glucksberg* that both New York and Washington states were not violating the constitution by allowing PAS. So Ashcroft chose to dodge the ruling by approaching it in another way—through the regulation of controlled substances. Thus he directed the Drug Enforcement Agency to proceed against Oregon physicians for dispensing life-ending medicines, a practice that the previous attorney general, Janet Reno, had ruled legal. It is important to realize that Ashcroft's challenge did not originate in the lower courts or with a groundswell of opposition, but was part of larger Bush administration efforts to bring religion into government, measures that included trying to obtain federal funds to pay for religious schools and church-run activities and to inculcate "family values" into the business of government through chastity programs in the public schools and the like. For those members of the disability community who consider themselves liberal or progressive, there was a distinct irony to supporting Ashcroft and Gonzales's agenda.

I'd like to rehearse and then rebut some of the arguments against PAS from within the disability community. One argument against PAS is based on the assumption that the medical community, combined with hospital administrations, insurance companies, and nursing homes, is eager to get the chance to euthanize people with disabilities or to pressure them into taking their own lives. Add to this the ableist world that puts dread in people's hearts about losing control, being disabled, and so on. The combination of increasingly limited resources, pressure from nondisabled people, and so on, it is believed, will lead to increased deaths of people with disabilities, particularly very dependent and disabled people. Disability studies, which to a certain extent came out of disability activism, is informed by the early battles in that cause. Activists have indeed cut their teeth fighting for the rights of people with disabilities who were made hopeless by prejudice and lack of resources and who wanted the state to euthanize them, people like Bouvia, Rivlin, MacAfee, and Bergstedt (all of whom were disabled, but none of whom were dying in the way specified by the Oregon law). And then there was the case of Terri Schiavo, which showed the horrors of the forced killing of a disabled woman. The mantra that came from these moments was that euthanasia, eugenics, and physician-assisted suicide were all part of the problem and that a united stand against them should be taken. This set of associations has remained largely unchallenged, except by the disability group Autonomy.

Reasonable folks who take this position insist that their temporary alliance with right-to-life groups and others holding distasteful political positions is only tactical and that there are major areas of disagreement—notably around abortion (although with the caveat that certain kinds of abortions—those with the aim of preventing a child being born with disabilities—may be problematic). But those distinctions are lost on the American public, who might come to see disability as increasingly associated with right-wing and religious causes, as happened in the Schiavo case. In addition, as I mentioned, each case of this kind weakens the impact of *Roe v. Wade*, which was decided purely on the right to privacy. *Griswold v. Connecticut* established a right to privacy in the bedroom, and *Lawrence v. Texas* gave a right to privacy in gay sexual relations. Do we in the disability community want to support legal decisions that might weaken this right to privacy in areas around control of one's body in an end-of-life scenario?

My feeling is that many in the disability community are going down their own slippery slope with their position. When you make alliances with groups that are in many ways your sworn enemy, there is a problem. When you stand up next to the American Medical Association, which opposes PAS, you have to ask why. And when you unthinkingly risk the very right to privacy that protects you against unwarranted governmental interference, you may well need to rethink that position.

Disability studies is fundamentally based, among other things, on the idea that people with disabilities should have autonomy over their own lives. The independent living movement and much disability legislation stress that barriers to active participation and self-determination should be removed. It is better to live at home with personal assistants, work without discrimination, navigate the streets without barriers, communicate by all means, use media and technology, than to be taken care of in facilities, confined to a home, limited by ableist technologies, and so on. While that appeal to autonomous identity may be tempered by a recognition that we are all interdependent, that the model of the free and autonomous individual is a bit of a myth, and that appeals to normality are hegemonic, autonomy over one's body is still a valuable idea.

Should one give up the notion of autonomy for a restrictive sense that one's identity as disabled trumps one's identity as a citizen with full human rights? How did disability activists and scholars get themselves into this paradoxical position?

As I mentioned, there are historical reasons for seeing PAS and euthanasia as connected. But it seems to me that the biggest problem comes in eliding the difference between the disability identity and the identity of a dying person. It is a particularly illogical move to envision all people who are dying as disabled. The faulty syllogism goes that dying people are disabled and that, in an ableist society, they will naturally be pressured to kill themselves; ergo, disabled people are being put to death. Further, those who make this argument feel that dying people (read "newly disabled" people) will ask for physician-assisted suicide specifically because they do not wish to be disabled, because they fear losing sight, hearing, voice, mobility, and so on. In other words, such people, while newly disabled, are in fact ableists, since they are the products of an ableist society. Thus we must stop these newly disabled people from being ableist.

There are several flaws in this argument. First, it is hard, although not impossible, to shoehorn someone dying of cancer into the category of chronic disability. The aim of living with one's impairment and having a free and accessible society has little to do with someone who will be dead in six months (the requirement for receiving PAS). Why should someone have to accept their disability status when they will have left this life by the time they get used to it? Second, according to the statistics provided by Oregon's annual report on PAS, the majority of people seeking PAS are end-stage cancer patients. The typical person asking for PAS is a white, seventy-two-year-old man, well educated, dying of cancer. Those requesting self-administered lethal overdoses are by and large educated, middle class, and informed.[4] They don't fit into the picture of the poor, disabled person of color being exterminated by a greedy medical-industrial complex.

A big issue for those disability activists who oppose PAS is that the main reasons given by terminal patients in Oregon for choosing PAS are fear of lost autonomy, loss of control, and dependency. This raises a red flag for people who have disabilities and for disability studies scholars and activists because it signals a major prejudice involved in ableism—the tendency to see normality and independence as a sine qua non of full personhood. Disability studies has taught us to critique those ableist assumptions.

While it is true that many seek PAS because they fear losing their abilities and their autonomy, they no doubt have a right to their fear and to the independent judgment to make this decision. Why should one group of morally or ethically like-minded people dictate whether a person can seek a legal overdose? I agree with seeing the need for autonomy and control as an aspect of ableism, but I believe that this attitude has to change through education, increased media involvement, and evolving public awareness. I don't think that people with disabilities (PWDs) can prohibit people from making choices even if those choices seem wrong to many PWDs. The extension of this logic would have to involve prohibiting advanced medical directives if they are motivated by the "wrong" attitudes. In other words, if means exist now for ending one's life through the use of advanced directives, the right to refuse treatment, the right to be sedated, and so on, why won't those rights be abused as well? Won't family pressure and discrimination against PWDs influence an advanced directive? By that same logic, then, we should not allow advanced directives.

To the general public, it will seem obviously illogical that disability advocates are in favor of preventing dying people from choosing a humane way of ending their lives because they see suicide as a critique of the disability perspective. While the religious right lumps PAS, euthanasia, and abortion together, a more nuanced position would want to make distinctions. But the history of the treatment of people with disabilities has made this impulse toward nuance difficult. A long history of abuse, culminating in eugenics and discrimination, has provided a clear oppressor to some people with disabilities. So ironically, a movement that began as an outgrowth of progressive disabled Vietnam veterans returning to demand proper treatment combined with liberal-to-left women from the feminist movement and people involved in the civil rights movement has come to the point where its major political statements involve making bedfellows with the religious right, the AMA, and social conservatives.

If a more nuanced discussion were to happen, or should happen, I would make several points. Arguments in the abstract are well and good, but we can't discuss whether PAS will lead to euthanasia of people with disabilities without looking at specific examples. To just state that a particular outcome is certain without adequate proof is not a wise course. The much favored slippery slope argument is considered illogical in rhetoric since no one can prove that his or her version of the slope is correct. You can have your slippery slope, and I can have mine, but neither of us can actually foresee the future. This inevitability of the slippery slope becomes less inevitable if you think of the antimarijuana argument and the anti–gay marriage argument as slippery slope ones.

And the facts do not bear out the slippery slope argument. The Oregon Death with Dignity Act has been in effect for thirteen years. In that time the total number of people per year who have used the law to kill themselves has risen from fifteen in the first year to sixty-eight in the thirteenth year. In the past three years the number per year has hovered around sixty. Given the total number of people in Oregon, these few people can hardly be said to constitute a landslide of people rolling toward death down a slippery slope.

Regarding the economic issue, the argument is that forced euthanasia will increase as economic times get hard and patients and their families are pressured to vacate hospital beds via suicide. However, it is hard to imagine that the AMA would oppose PAS if they could make a lot of money off of it. In reality, very few people have chosen the PAS option in Oregon. Sixty people would not generate the big bucks the medical establishment is looking for to balance its books. The majority of these people were not in nursing homes or hospitals, so the argument that PAS frees up extra beds seems unlikely. Indeed most people using PAS died at home (97 percent this year) or in a hospice. The argument that the poor and people of color will be disproportionately singled out for PAS is also dubious, considering that 100 percent of the people who used assisted suicide this year were white. And they were generally well educated and middle class.

It is understandable that we might make the analogy and say that if the poor and marginalized generally get inferior health care, then they are the most likely to be killed as a result of a PAS regime. But the data do not bear out this assumption. How can we make sense of the data then? We can ignore it, or we can say that in fact PAS does not represent inadequate or failed health care, but actually top-of-the-line intervention. PAS is the option chosen by the wealthy, educated, dominant, even gender-dominant group. In addition, institutionally it is most often provided in a hospice setting, which is the top-of-the-line choice for people who are dying. Hospices also are the leaders in providing palliative care, so it seems to be a major misunderstanding to assume that poor palliative care leads to a decision to use PAS. Rather, the opposite seems true.[5]

There is, in fact, a deep contradiction in the anti-PAS position, in this regard. Take Marilyn Golden's point that

the very small number of people who may benefit from legalizing assisted suicide will tend to be affluent, white, and in possession of good health insurance coverage. At the same time, large numbers of people, particularly among those less privileged in society, would be at significant risk of harm.[6]

On the one hand, PAS is seen as something that rich people want, and at the same time it is seen as something that poor people shouldn't want. But if it benefits affluent, white people, why won't it benefit all people? In the distribution of privileges and services in society, our goal should be to provide equal benefits regardless of race, class, disability, and so on.

Opponents of PAS point to the Netherlands as their netherworld experience.[7] People claim that the Netherlands can act as an experiment telling us what to expect and that what we see there is a fulfillment of slippery slope predictions. But the data do not support this claim, and the interpretation of the data is also significant. It is important to understand that the Netherlands experience is quite different from the US experience in many ways. First, over 80 percent of the citizenry in the Netherlands supports euthanasia and PAS.[8] The United States has a dramatically lower rate of approval. The culture of the Netherlands is very different from US culture. Prostitution, for example, is legal in the Netherlands, as is marijuana usage. It is hard to imagine the US citizenry rallying for such progressive measures, and there is little chance that the Dutch experience will become the US experience.

Nevertheless, it is worth considering some of the criticisms of Holland's practices and laws. Herbert Hendin points to the fact that euthanasia is performed routinely by doctors in Holland, even on people who did not request an end-of-life intervention.[9] The implication is that creating laws favoring PAS will lead to more and more people (particularly people with disabilities, poor people, senior citizens, people of color, and so on) being killed by doctors, who will grow more and more used to the life-ending privilege. But several points need to be considered. First, in the Netherlands neither race, class, nor disability status seems to factor into the quality of health care because all people are covered by a cradle-to-grave national health system.[10] Second, there have been no demonstrations in the Netherlands against end-of-life procedures by citizens with disabilities in the thirty years that euthanasia has been allowed.[11] In fact, the Netherlands is the most studied country in regard to its end-of-life practices, and although, for example, a very low percentage of physicians euthanizing patients without their permission is found, that percentage is actually much lower than in countries that do not allow euthanasia, including Belgium, Denmark, Italy, and Sweden.[12] We can speculate that in the United States,

PAS is occurring illegally in many states, not just legally in Oregon, Washington, and Montana, but since we do not require physicians to report all such deaths, it would be difficult to say what the actual rate might be.

We might want to be aware that in the United States, almost all anti-PAS sentiment from the Netherlands is filtered through Dr. Herbert Hendin. He has a strong agenda as the director of the American Society for Suicide Prevention, is highlighted on the website of the National Right to Life organization, and testified before George W. Bush's conservative Bioethics Commission (the same outfit that refused to allow stem cell research).[13] I don't say that all his information is biased, but we need to consider his overall project. If you oppose suicide at all costs, it is obvious you will oppose PAS.[14]

Given his dramatic bias, even Hendin admits that the suicide rate in the Netherlands has dropped dramatically and that, remarkably, the number of people requesting PAS has not risen, particularly as palliative care has been made more important in Dutch medical practice. He, of all people, should be emphasizing the slippery slope argument, but the Netherlands experience does not bear this out. Here are Hendin's own bullet points concerning the Netherlands in response to the US Bioethics Commission:

- No increase in assisted suicide and euthanasia cases from 1995 to 2001, compared to 20 percent increase between 1991–1995.
- If educational program is successful, this will be reflected in a decrease in the number of cases of assisted suicide and euthanasia.[15]

Another area of concern has been that the Netherlands was not using palliative care to help dying people. Without a program of hospices and palliative care, the argument goes, dying people will suffer more and therefore request PAS at higher rates. If you take care of pain, you won't need PAS. The Netherlands, however, has increased its palliative care measures dramatically.[16] And requests for PAS based on fear of future suffering are not considered valid in the Netherlands. In fact, only two out of five requests for PAS are honored in the Netherlands.[17]

The Oregon and Washington laws are not perfect. Neither is the ADA or the applications of *Roe vs. Wade*. Laws aren't about being perfect; they are about defining how things should go under general circumstances. Our aim should be to insure that the laws work better, not that there be no laws at all. And the alternative to laws is no law—which is the case now in most states. Under the present conditions, given general practice, assisted suicide with and without permission happens every day. People kill themselves with the help of doctors, friends, and family, only without a law the helpers risk jail terms and, even if they are not prosecuted, feel a sense of criminality, guilt, and shame. It would be better to require disclosure and compliance to a set of regulations than to leave things to the Wild West of ethics that operates today.

One way to understand the unreasonableness of the disability anti-PAS position is to perform a thought experiment. What if we insisted that any PAS law must contain the following proviso: "No one with a disability can be a candidate for physician-assisted suicide." That would take care of any objection that PWDs could be unduly pressured into killing themselves. But the obvious point would be that this would also deprive PWDs of the same right or option that everyone else had. Such a restriction would be discriminatory and violate the Equal Protection Clause of the Eleventh Amendment. The point is that if you think it is unfair to give this right or option to the general public but withhold it from a person with a disability, then you must feel that the option has some validity.

And this is perhaps the crux of what I am trying to say. To have a disability is to have one part of a multistranded identity. Of course a person with a disability might develop a fatal disease. The disability and the disease are not necessarily connected to each other definitionally or in any other way. In some cases PWDs who are dying of cancer and other diseases might not have the access or ability to kill themselves. They might want to ask a friend or family member for help but also might fear asking that person to commit a crime. People with amyotrophic lateral sclerosis (ALS), for example, face this set of decisions from the moment they are diagnosed since a difficult death is certain. They have a few options, and one of them is PAS. ALS websites contain pages on trying to decide whether to go on a ventilator and then die or to opt for an earlier death before the attritions that inevitably will lead to death.

It has been argued that the Oregon law is flawed for several reasons. One is that compliance is flimsy. In fact, in 2011, eighty-three people died from ingesting medication—of those eighty-one were fully reported and two were not, which is a 97-percent compliance rate. If that rate is not acceptable, then the answer to is to give such laws more teeth. But the danger of that move is that under Health Insurance Portability and Accountability Act (HIPAA) regulations, strict limits are set on access to patients' records. Stricter laws might violate HIPAA regulations. And there is a more general question about whether committing suicide is an act protected by the right to privacy. For example, should we require that all abortion clinics and physicians keep data on everyone and report this to the local authorities? We generally feel that private acts of great emotional and physical risk should not be made part of the public record. And currently, in non-PAS states, there is no way of knowing whether a physician assisted a patient in dying, while at least PAS laws require some level of compliance and disclosure.

Another objection to death-with-dignity laws is that it is difficult or impossible to say whether a person has only six months to live. While it is true that there is no absolute ability to predict such things, it is also true that most of these predictions are relatively accurate. The anti-PAS side often cites medical reports to the effect that such predictions are impossible to make, but if you actually look at the articles cited by anti-PAS critics, they come from nonmedical, non-peer-reviewed journals, and they often misquote, partially quote, or even completely change the sense of the original article. The fairest thing to say is that prediction is not an exact science, but, given that caveat, predictions can have a fair degree of accuracy. In fact, one article cited on a "myth/fact sheet" opposing PAS actually concedes that there is accuracy within a week between prediction and death and that this prediction can be made even more accurate by including other factors.[18] The point is that the six-month requirement is put there to indicate that the person has a fatal disease and will die of it within a short time. If the exact prediction were off by a week or even a few months, the general outcome or scope of the problem would not change substantially.

Objections are also made that the person requesting the assistance may be depressed and should be treated for the depression, not given lethal drugs. Linked to this is the assertion that the Oregon law as it now stands doesn't *really* screen for depression even though it requires an assessment for depression. This line of reasoning works well for the subject of euthanasia, especially for a disabled person who is depressed by living situation, lack of access, accommodation, and so on. But in the case of someone who is dying, the point is a bit moot. Must there be Pollyannas on every cancer ward? Must dying people be cheerful? What is the point of treating end-stage cancer patients for depression when they say that they have determined they want to die? Therapeutics get mixed up with ethics here, and people with disabilities should be the ones most sensitive to this act of medicalization. This is not to say that the psychological state of people who are dying should be disregarded, but it might equally be true that extensive interviewing to determine if the dying person is really depressed or just depressed because they are dying can seem a hair-splitting, not to say cruel, exercise. Oregon physicians report that 20 percent of patients requesting PAS were depressed, but no depressed patients received a lethal prescription. Depression among all dying patients ranges from 10 to 25 percent; those requesting PAS are no more or less depressed than the general dying population.[19]

It is possible for a reasoned debate of this issue to take place within disability studies, and it is most important that all factors are taken into consideration. A simple up or down declaration of faith in PAS or against it amounts to little more than a conviction—based on fact or not. I am hopeful that disability studies, in the richness and fullness of its contribution to society at large, will not pass up the opportunity to articulate these crucial issues by substituting simple reflex and assumption for consistent thought and reason. We can all agree on some aspects of our field—that people with disability are oppressed, that negative representations of people with disabilities have abounded in the past and continue to do so, and so on. But then there are the areas that we cannot and may never find a single answer to—we might include the validity of prenatal genetic testing and the abortion of disabled fetuses. In that category must be the complex and ethically challenging issue of PAS. For disability studies to take a reasoned stance on this issue means that it must accede to difference of opinion within the disability community. Although a group of scholars and activists are very certain that PAS is wrong at all costs, their opinion must be brought into dialogue with a spectrum of beliefs, feelings, convictions, and arguments provided by others.

And it is my opinion that a reasoned consideration will end up seeing that the sentiments, methods, and convictions behind banning PAS are contrary to the kind of world disability studies envisions we should all inhabit. Further, I believe that PAS is part of a progressive agenda supported by those who have developed fair and accountable notions of justice, rights, and citizenship in democracies. I also welcome the fact that others may disagree with my position since it is only through argument and debate that we can find, if not the truth, then the information behind what may be truth.

CHAPTER EIGHT

Transgendered Freud

In speaking of identity as biocultural, I want to emphasize the link between body, mind, and culture. Among the newest identities coming into social consciousness are ones related to transgender, and the roots of that identity both go deep into history and culture and yet seem relatively new. One place people have rarely looked to find origins is in the work of Freud, who seemed, perhaps until recently, to be not the founder of sexual identities but the confounder. In this essay, I want to try to reclaim Freud by thinking of him as a daring and early advocate of a gender continuum.

In 1876 Freud began his career when he was nineteen by dissecting eels to try to find the male gonad. It was a difficult task and ended in failure. Freud wrote to his friend Wilhelm Fleiss, saying, "I obtain sharks, rays, eels and other creatures, which I investigate first from the general anatomical viewpoint and thereafter with regard to one particular problem." The problem was "since time immemorial, only the female [eel] has been recognized; even Aristotle did not know where the male of the species was." Freud chose to explore this seeming transgender animal that was possibly hermaprohodite, possibly a parthenogenetic example of how females could reproduce without males. He went on to say, "one does not know which is male and which is female when the animal does not possess external sexual differences." He notes that if you can't find gonads and you can't find secondary sex characteristics, then you won't be able to figure out which eel is male or female "since eels do not keep diaries." But Freud ended up failing in his attempts: "Now I am toiling to rediscover this eel, this male eel; but in vain, all the eels I cut open are of the fairer sex." To this comment he adds a drawing of a somewhat demure and fetching female eel (see fig. 1).

Fig. 1

Freud is obviously trying to establish traditional reproductive categories on this seemingly aberrant eel.[1]

That Freud should have begun his career this way is too good a gift for a biocultural critic to pass up. The obvious insight is that the eel, itself a kind of phallic symbol, was paradoxically only known to be female. The young Freud obviously took to eels with a certain fascination and began to gender them in anthropomorphic ways, as his drawing shows. Yet even as he draws a female eel, he wants to anatomize it and find a male sexual organ within it. He is hoping that the female eel will yield a testicle rather than an ovary.

This anatomizing of the eel's body is significant in a number of ways. Sander Gilman and others have shown how during Freud's era, Jews were considered feminized compared with other Europeans. Complex issues around racial categories and circumcision led the Jewish man's body to contain both a masculine and a feminine element—masculine because the circumcised penis is the hidden identifier of Jewish maleness and feminine because the penis is altered or even castrated, vulnerable, and diminished. Gilman points to Freud's attempt to find the inner male in the outwardly female eel as part of his Jewish self-analysis.[2] The eel analogy is furthered because Jews and Romas were apparently compared to eels, who wander through the oceans of the world as these ethnic groups were thought to wander the planet.

Freud's failure to find the male gonad in the eel caused him to reassess the whole notion of a fixed biological determinism and propelled him from biology to the psyche. In this new course of study, Freud's notions of gender deemphasized the purely physical genitals and emphasized their meanings, signification, and import to the individual. In this sense, he was engaging in a kind of early transbiology, which according to Sarah Franklin includes the notion of the cultural meanings inherent in the "facts" of biology.[3] Rather than stressing a genetic inheritance, Freud elaborated a series of developmental instances from infant to child to adult that would nominate one's sexual orientation and gender identity, rather than some biological fixity, a hard-to-find or elusive gonad hidden in the recesses of the body.

An essential part of Freud's new theory of sexuality was that humans are bisexual in nature. He was no longer trying to find a binary in the sex of eels or humans, but rather to allow a dialectic of admixtures. Freud wrote in 1899 to his friend Wilhelm Fliess, who first suggested the idea: "Bisexuality! I am sure you are right about it. And I am accustoming myself to regarding every sexual act as an event between four individuals."[4] In 1905, Freud wrote, "Without taking bisexuality into account I think it would scarcely be possible to arrive at an understanding of the sexual manifestations that are actually to be observed in men and women."[5]

As with the eels, then, it would be fruitless to try and locate human gender identity in the purely biological. Freud said in a public lecture, addressing an audience that he assumed regarded gender as obvious, "When you meet a human being, the first distinction you make is 'male or female' and you are accustomed to make the distinction with unhesitating certainty." But Freud then queers this idea, noting that "science . . . draws your attention to the fact that portions of the male sexual apparatus also appear in women's bodies, although in an atrophied state, and vice versa in the alternative case." He goes on to say that science "regards their occurrence as indications of *bisexuality*, as though an individual is not a man or a woman but always both—merely a certain amount more the one than the other." His final point is that "what constitutes masculinity and femininity is an unknown characteristic which anatomy cannot lay hold of."[6]

Notably, here Freud points to an "unknown characteristic," which is not anatomy, that determines gender. What could this "unknown characteristic" be? Freud observed that many might suppose this characteristic to be something socially determined—something like being "active" or "passive." But he quickly nixes that proposition, noting, "it seems to serve no useful purpose and adds nothing to our knowledge."[7] Further, he uncouples the sex drive itself from gender: "There is only one libido, which serves both the masculine and feminine sexual functions. To it itself we cannot assign any sex."[8] Freud is often quoted as saying that "Anatomy is Destiny," but the reality is that Freud believed that Libido is Destiny, and he offers a very serendipitous notion of destiny.

The essence of how we develop into gendered subjects is located in Freud's idea of the Oedipal complex. The stereotypical and reductionist way of thinking of this famous or notorious complex is that it serves to fix, rather than queer, gender lines. For Freud, though, the complex is a way of talking about the intersection of the cultural, social, moral world and the individual's entrance into those politics. In effect, he says that there is no biological determinism involved, since each child will have to deal with that "unknown characteristic" within (and this will involve a bisexual origin, a tendency on the part of the child toward some admixture of male and female) and then with the cultural, religious, moral, and structural necessity for the child to renounce the bisexuality (and the admixture) for some socially acceptable and recognizable gender identity.

Freud is often accused of having a simple view of gender, but in reality the permutations and combinations of the binaries involved in the Oedipal complex are truly staggering. Freud points out that "the simple Oedipus complex is by no means its commonest form, but rather represents a simplification. Indeed the complex form of the complex is more the rule: a boy has not merely an ambivalent attitude towards his father and an affectionate object-choice towards his mother, but at the same time he also behaves like a girl and displays an affectionate feminine attitude to his father and a corresponding jealousy and hostility toward his mother. It is this complicating element introduced by bisexuality that makes it so difficult to obtain a clear view of the facts in connection with the earliest object choices and identifications."[9] The result of the resolution of the complex is that one's gender identity, made through "choices and identifications," may become stereotypical if "successful." But the maleness or femaleness that ensues is deeply part of what Lacan calls "misrecognition," since the pure essence of maleness or femaleness is dubious. All humans "as a result of their bisexual disposition . . . , combine in themselves both masculine and feminine characteristics, so that pure masculinity and femininity remain theoretical constructions of uncertain content." Like the "uncertain characteristic" that determines gender, the outcome—that is, the socially acceptable gender—is "of uncertain content." For Freud gender itself has a certain incommensurability to it. Masculinity is something socially constructed, and "the majority of men are far behind the masculine ideal."[10] As with the eel, one is unlikely to find an anatomical substrate that will determine all. Neither can one locate or point to gender as distinctly knowable or present.

Like the unconscious, gender is amorphous, difficult to fix or even decipher. For Freud gender involves a psychical calculus that combines a genital Imaginary with the erotics of object choice. So whether a person chooses as sexual partners men, women, or both, there is no major distinction, since all are part of this calculus. Freud is interested in describing variations in human sexuality without making judgments. Once you perform the transbiological action of divorcing sexuality from "too close connection with the genitals" and locating it in a matrix of cultural and social norms, then desire becomes the major motive, as Freud notes, and so sexuality has "pleasure as its goal and only secondarily coming to serve the ends of reproduction."[11] Freud is not impressed by the old Darwinian saw of distinct gender divisions as sanctioned by evolution for the ultimate goal of reproduction. Freud points out in *Three Essays on Sexuality* that if reproduction were the only purpose of sexuality, then kissing, foreplay, and other aspects of sexual play would not have evolved because they detract from the specific activity of insemination.[12] In Freud's scheme, the discharge of libido, that is, pleasure and instinctual gratification, is paramount, while reproduction is secondary. Given this emphasis on pleasure, varieties of sexual choice including homosexuality are then "normal," since these are "found in people who exhibit no other serious deviations from the normal." Because homosexuality is found in people "distinguished by specially high intellectual development and ethical culture," it is even better than normal. And the fact "that some of the most prominent men in all recorded history were homosexuals, as well as the entire culture of Ancient Greece . . . make[s] it impossible to regard" homosexuality "as a sign of degeneracy."[13] Indeed, it could be regarded as a sign of genius and superiority.

But it is perhaps Freud's discovery or institutionalization of childhood sexuality that creates the space for an ontology of the sexual subject. This ontology has very little to do with which configuration of genitals a child may have—Freud consigns that aspect of binary determinism to biology, which he now wants to augment with psychology. So, it isn't the genitals but the psychic representation of the genitals that is most important. And by giving children sexuality, Freud establishes that one's gender orientation is the product of incidents and accidents that occur in early childhood. The development of the child, from an initial polymorphous perversity with its first love object as the breast, through the anal phase, latency, and then the genital phase, allows for many stations along the way in which sexuality can find its particular desires and pleasures. In the beginning, Freud postulates a subject-object dialectic formed by the infant's linking the breast to the mother, who through her care becomes the subject's "first seducer."[14] The steps involved in the Oedipus complex create hall-of-mirror images and imagos endlessly reflecting different admixtures of gender identity. Fixations at various phases of development can shape the aims of each individual and his or her object choices. In other words, a combination of some very nuanced kind of individual agency together with chance occurrences and the general overall shape of human development produces a sexual being with specific desires, object choices, and ambivalences.

Along the way, the formation of gender is deeply tied to the cultural necessity that the binary of bisexuality be repressed in favor of a single sexual orientation. In *Civilization and Its Discontents,* Freud notes that society and culture at large impose such restrictions on sexuality. "In this respect civilization behaves towards sexuality as a people or a stratum of its population does which has subjected another one to its exploitation." Political repression and sexual repression are analogous, and Freud notes with dismay that "as regards the sexually mature individual, the choice of an object is restricted to the opposite sex. . . . The requirement demonstrated in these prohibitions, that there shall be a single kind of sexual life for everyone, disregards the dissimilarities, whether innate or acquired, in the sexual constitution of human beings; it cuts off a fair number of them from sexual enjoyment, and so becomes the source of serious injustice."[15]

Yet it is only with dynamic repression of various unacceptable (to society, family, the law, culture) options that the unconscious is formed. The unconscious, then, in my reading of Freud, is actually the space of gendering and ungendering—which only becomes the publicly assigned gender by its reliance on the repudiated gender or gender admixture. Given a Lacanian reading of this notion, gender is then a form of *meconnaisance*—misrepresentation. In this sense, the publicly identified gender is always the product of a repression and then a redeployment of sexuality—which then means paradoxically that one's gender is defined in the place where one's gender is not. The unconscious is the place where one really "is"—it is the place of authenticity—but it is forever inaccessible to the publicly gendered subject and available only by indirect observation. It would be a fantastical dress-up room in which gender parts and aspects freely float around in random, dreamlike order.

One interesting refinement of this idea results from the fact that Freud actually never used the terms *ego* or *id* but rather, in German, "Das Ich" and "Das Es," which translate as the "I" and the "It." It was only Freud's English translators, the Stracheys, who wanted to make Freud more scientific sounding to impress the skeptical Anglo-American medical establishment. Interestingly, the unconscious is the "It," the other to the "I." Tellingly, neither of these pronouns is gendered. Both are in fact grammatically "neuter," and so we might say that the "I" of the subject, while publicly gendered in some specular sense, is really not where gender resides. Rather, gender resides in the object, the It, itself a repository of repressed gender imagos.

One's gender is always, then, in the other—even if the other is one's own (unconscious) self. Another way of saying this is that gender is not subject; rather, it is object.

Likewise, in the Lacanian sense, the phallus is not a gender determinant, but a referential marker of power and activity. This power is in effect the cause that influences the infant to make choices and engage in trying to shape the incidents and accidents of its nascent sexual life into some narrative, some representation, that can get it through the barriers and allow a complex gendered self to emerge. The adult subject, then, becomes the inauthentic, simplified, publicly gendered self, while the core of ontological being is the location of the It; one's gender, like the phallus, is therefore more about a certain kind of instrumental usage than about some authentic biological determination. Inside every "man" or "woman" therefore is the inaccessible and unaccountable space of the "It."

Because those very social, moral, and political forces extend deep into early childhood through the agency of the family with its legitimizing structures and punishments, every person's ontology is conditioned less by phylogeny than by structures of social and political power. Thus, the famously controversial "castration anxiety" is Freud's way of talking about the threat of violence menacing the free choice of gender or sexuality in childhood. While one may want to repudiate the sheer maleness of the model produced (with its attendant "penis envy"), a Lacanian reading has been sufficient to shift the notion of the penis as biological artifact to the phallus as biocultural fact of power and control.

A final question remains to determine the nature of the subject whose sexual ontology we are considering. Freud does posit, in the midst of his social construction of gender, that there is some anterior self—what he earlier called that "unknown characteristic"—that precedes the formation of the unconscious and that precedes the individual accidents of childhood sexuality. This inchoate proto-self Freud describes as having some predilection toward gender admixture. Each person may have some preference toward masculinity or femininity that each subject prepossesses (before one can in any sense be said to possess) in some way that is neither prepossessing nor abject. It is also important to note that Freud does not postulate masculinity and femininity in any clear way. Freud speaks of "the opposition between two currents, which runs through all sexual life." These cannot be described as "'masculine' and 'feminine, but only as 'active' and 'passive.'"[16] Freud mentions several times that the very concept of masculine and feminine is problematic because it can't be linked to biology (since we are biological admixtures with homologous organs) or to culture (since there is so much variety in culture and since cultures differ). In *Civilization and Its Discontents* he comments, "though anatomy, it is true, can point out the characteristic of maleness and femaleness, psychology cannot. For psychology the contrast between the sexes fades away into one between activity and passivity."[17] It is important to remember that Freud had already said that a simple equation of active and male and passive and female is incorrect. Perhaps active would loosely correspond to "top" as passive would correspond to "bottom." These are choice positions and yet not entirely chosen, certainly not biological, influenced by culture but not isolated to any of those factors.

Freud says that all sexuality is based on remembering. "The finding of an object is in fact a refinding of it."[18] When we touch the other, when we kiss and suck, when we engage in sexual contact and fetishize parts of the body or objects connected with the body, we are remembering our earliest experiences of the erotic. But those memories themselves are hallucinations of some earlier unrecordable, nonlinguistic physical and emotional contact. We can't actually remember being at the breast; we can only remember the memory of pleasure and the rehallucination of the supposed event. It is in those unremembered acts that the rudiments of gender and object choice were formed. Gender and object choice may be disconnected on some profound level, but for Freud they are also connected—not categorically, but affectively—and bounded by memory.

With memory, there is both agency and the absence of agency. For Freud there is no forgetting, and even the act of forgetting is itself an act of remembering. When we forget a name or an act or a word, we are remembering something that actively prevents us from completing the memory, as he points out in *The Psychopathology of Everyday Life*. In that sense, if gender is formed from the residues of memory—both psychic and body memory—it is at once active in the sense of being constructed from those parts and passive in the sense of being shaped by the past. While one can choose in some existential way what to recall and what to forget, the forgetting is never entirely willed since it is held in the thrall of a nonconscious repression, an act of repression not immediately knowable by the self. So the notion of agency involved in the creation of gender is this very specific kind of actively passive subjectivity.

Thus, the Ur state of knowing the self is inchoate and, in a sense, given, although never merely biological. What could it be? It is something archaic or primitive in the mind—perhaps simply a preference, a tendency—that becomes the armature for a later knowing self (always with the proviso that the self that one knows is the mistaken self of the ego). Perhaps Freud comes as close as he ever does to some idea of a "given" in personality, which, while not deterministic, is at least a compromise with sheer randomness and chance. The trans-Freud I have been trying to find gives us the dual message that gender is both a product of a developmental process conditioned by power in its broadest and most particular senses and a *donee*, a given, which is itself, if not a fact, then at least a possibility toward expressivity. To queer Judith Butler's term, it is not so much performance as pre-formance—a state of choice before the possibility for choosing. This active passivity that is subjectivized before subjectivity seems to be the site of this choosing that is a prechoosing. In that ambiguous seed of identity, the spinning out of transpossibilities can begin and so paradoxically provide an end in sight, with all the attendant complexities of that end.

What I've tried to do thus far is provide us with a new trans-Freud. It's not so much new as it is renewed, since Freud was clearly very aware of and foundational to a notion of gender as continuous and malleable. He remained committed throughout his life and career to opposing a hereditary-based or biologically rooted explanation of gender. He was unwaveringly committed to a bisexual view of human existence in a culture that would have found such an explanation anathema.

It might be appropriate also to note here that Freud's positionality as a Jew might have influenced his discussions of gender. Like his idea of gender, Freud's Jewishness is not bound to his body like a genital or inscribed on it with a circumcision. Freud rarely wrote about himself as a Jew, and yet, like the issue of gender, where he is not is where he is. He is not Jewish in his writing or in his body per se, but Jewishness is a religion that dare not say its name, especially in Germany and Austria. Freud was acutely aware of anti-Semitism in Vienna and in the university system. In one of his earliest memories, he describes walking with his father along the street and seeing his father accosted by a man who knocked his father's hat onto the sidewalk. Freud was saddened by his father's inability to stand up to the anti-Semite.[19] Freud was of a generation of young professionals who saw themselves as secular Jews but Jews nonetheless. Yet there was nothing biological about Freud's Jewish body. If he was Jewish, where was he Jewish? In this sense, Freud may have seen the unaccountability of gender to be connected with the unaccountability of his Jewishness.

I hope that I have presented a believable account of Freud as the first scientific articulator of note for a transgendered biology. Yet Freud's sexual politics are probably the most significant problem in arguing for a trans-Freud. The central issue here concerns the Oedipal complex, castration anxiety, penis envy, and the myth of vaginal orgasm. Freud argued that boys and girls are essentially the same in the first three years of life. He postulated that young children all think of themselves as having penises, as all being boys, since girls use and regard their clitorises as homologues to the penis. When young children become aware of biological difference, they attribute a motive to this difference. For Freud the implication was that children will hazard the guess that girls must have been boys whose penises were cut off. Why were they castrated? They were castrated because fathers are the angry and powerful possessors of penises who would punish with the ultimate penalty any child who claimed a primary place in the mother's affections. The resolution of the problem of the Oedipal conflict is that girls identify with their mothers, gaining strength from the identification, which would displace their feelings of loss from penis to future childbearing. Boys identify with their fathers, gaining the power of the father and the security of being an ally, not a rival. When puberty comes, boys take on the role of penis bearers fairly easily. For girls, the active attachment to the clitoris for masturbatory pleasure has to be transferred to the vagina, which is the organ of use for a mature woman intent on marriage and childbirth.

There is much wrong in this theory, although I would argue that there is much right, and right in a queer sense. Initially, it might be helpful to realize that when Freud came up with his theories, sexology was in its infancy. Freud and others were obsessed with wondering whether there is a biological basis for sexuality and gender. But post-eel Freud was less interested in biology and more interested in the psychic and symbolic role played by the biological. For example, neither Freud nor his contemporaries were aware of sexual hormones (or any hormones) when *Three Essays on Sexuality* was published in 1905. Insulin was discovered in 1922, estrogen in 1925, and testosterone in 1935. Freud actually anticipates their discovery by saying that there must be some substance circulating in the blood that accounts for sexual feelings and orientation. Another rather surprising example is that it was not until 1925 that the female human ovum was seen and that the exact cycle of a woman's fertility was established. Doctors previously believed that women were fertile only during their periods, as dogs were during estrus. So it shouldn't surprise us that Freud's discussion of the biology of sexuality might be very different from ours. As Freud says at one point, "It must be admitted, however, that in general our insight into these developmental processes in girls is unsatisfactory, incomplete and vague."[20] In fact, the average high school student knows much more about sexuality and reproduction than did Freud and his contemporaries.

The primacy that Freud gives the clitoris is perhaps a more surprising revelation. To many people at the time a woman was indeed a man without a penis, and clitorises were not commonly written or talked about. The *OED* lists no common usages of the term. *My Secret Life*, a pornographic memoir published in 1902, uses the term, but earlier works like *Fanny Hill* only use metaphoric language. Thomas Lacquer notes that as early as the seventeenth century the clitoris had been observed and described anatomically, but without the anatomical term being used. Freud's frank and free use of the term and his assertion that the clitoris is in fact like a penis are noteworthy. Girls, according to Freud, have small penises and boys larger ones. As Freud writes, "In her childhood . . . a girl's clitoris takes on the role of a penis entirely: it is characterized by special excitability and is the area in which auto-erotic satisfaction is obtained."[21] We also might want to note that Freud's reference to the clitoris, and his making it the prime organelle in a woman's sexual repertoire, is probably a positive step forward. According to Lucy Bland, most educated people were unfamiliar with the term, and in a 1918 trial in London, in which a woman was accused of being part of the "cult of the clitoris," Lord Albermarle was understood to have said, "I've never heard of this Greek chap Clitoris they are all talking of."[22]

As for the myth of the vaginal orgasm, Freud actually writes very little about it. His main point is that in "the process of a girl's becoming a woman" the clitoris passes "on this sensitivity to the vaginal orifice in good time and completely."[23] Obviously Freud's knowledge of female anatomy and sexuality is wrong, as was everyone's knowledge of everyone's sexuality at this time. What Freud is trying to reckon with is that in his society and culture the stereotypical role for women was to bear and rear children. Sexual intercourse for that aim obviously involves a woman's vagina centrally. So it would seem hopeful, for the culture of that era, that for successful reproduction to occur, a woman would have to find pleasure in the vagina. Yet Freud observes that a girl's seat of sexuality is her clitoris—hence the problem of how to make the transition. It didn't occur to Freud that clitorises can be stimulated in sexual intercourse or that vaginas might have sexual pleasures on their own—indeed, that debate continued through the 1980s over the validity of the now-accepted G-spot. Even today the argument for the evolutionary role of the female orgasm as a reward for sexual intercourse is itself a shaky one.[24]

Freud's logic simply follows the general themes we have observed. He sees sexuality as malleable, not dependent on biology per se. If boys and girls are essentially the same, and maleness and femaleness are more accurately thought of as activity and passivity, then the quantum of pleasure that resides in the clitoris can easily migrate to another part of the body. Indeed, for Freud, body parts can come psychically to stand in for other parts through sublimation, symbolization, cathexis, and the like. He is not saying that a woman is only a woman if she has vaginal pleasure. He is saying that in his society, a woman who does not find pleasure in sexual intercourse will be in trouble. She will certainly be unhappy as well as perhaps neurotic.

Much the same can be said of the Oedipal complex. It is a system devised to account for the social and cultural gender roles of fin de siecle Viennese society. If there are such categories as male and female in society, how do individuals grow into those categories? Freud's argument is not based on biology, as we have seen, but on each child doing what Freud calls "researches." And as Freud points out, each child as a researcher is essentially a lone scholar. At the tender age of three or four a child must come up with a theory of sexuality, an explanation for the birth of babies, and a way of thinking about his or her organs and the pleasures derived from them. That children get things wrong is no surprise—whether the thing wrong is the presence or absence of penises or the thing wrong is the motives and sexual activities of parents. Freud envisions and describes a master plan, but his daily work in his office is really more about the variations and deviations on that theme. Each young person must act as his or her own scientific researcher, guide, anatomical dummy, therapist, and narrator—the data derived and the interpretation related about it amount to the formation of one's gender and sex roles. What the Oedipus complex adds to a notion of transbiology is precisely that anatomy is *not* destiny. That much-quoted sentence from Freud was actually Freud's variation on Napoleon's notion that "character is destiny." Freud's changing of Napoleon's statement reiterates that Freud believes in character but sees character not in anatomy, as a crude deterministic thing, but as something that complexly attaches itself to biology. Freud should have probably said that "anatomy is the signifier of destiny." Symptoms, neurosis, gender, dreams, jokes, slips—all of these are the physical significations of the dynamically repressed unconscious. The unconscious can only manifest itself through the physical, through the body. But analysis can never be of the body but must always be how the unconscious uses the body as a sign-system. The body therefore, like the dream, is a kind of rebus that must be decoded. Gender is not destiny, but it is the self's destiny to have a body and for that body to be gendered or named in some gendered way. As with language, the manifestation of the unconscious will always have to have a physical form. It is in that particular sense, I believe, that Freud meant that anatomy was destiny. And if anatomy is destiny in that way, then it isn't destiny at all.

CHAPTER NINE

The Biocultures Manifesto

(cowritten with David Morris)

It was still a radical premise when *New Literary History*, in which this chapter first appeared, stated in 1969 that the analysis of literature needed to consider history and culture. The stand-alone, value-free model of New Criticism made earlier attempts to historicize literature or to place specific literary works in their cultural context seem old-fashioned. Today, by contrast, it is commonplace to see literary texts illuminated through a study of history and culture, while numerous theoretical perspectives, from feminisms to cognitive poststructuralism, have enriched our understanding of both history and culture. Literary history, in this sense, lends itself to continuous reinvention. So at the beginning of the twenty-first century, we make a new (but perhaps in a while old) and counterintuitive (but perhaps destined to be commonplace) proposal: that culture and history must be rethought with an understanding of their inextricable, if highly variable, relation to biology. The general name for this phenomenon we call "biocultures."

Biology—serving at times as a metaphor for science—is as intrinsic to the embodied state of readers and of writers as history and culture are intrinsic to the professional bodies of knowledge known as science and biology. To think of science without including a historical and cultural analysis would be like thinking of the literary text without the surrounding and embedding weave of discursive knowledges active or dormant at particular moments. It is similarly limited to think of literature—or to engage in debate concerning its properties or existence—without considering the network of meanings we might learn from a scientific perspective.

Combined, these propositions link with a more synthetic argument: that the biological without the cultural, or the cultural without the biological, is doomed to be reductionist at best and inaccurate at worst. Make no mistake; we are not aiming to revive the so-called (or Sokal-ed) science wars. The aim of that moment falsely pitted social constructionism against science. Social constructionism is self-limited and inaccurate if it implies that social facts may be entirely dissociated from biological facts. We seek instead, for their mutual benefit, to join the biological and the cultural.

At the outset, this aim will seem most alien to the two groups who most need it—humanists and scientists. Humanists may respond that they are doing very well, thank you, without needing to clog their intellectual arteries with discussions of functional magnetic resonance imaging technologies and debates about the future of the human genome. It will seem obvious to them that reading *Paradise Lost* could hardly require knowledge of the circulatory system or the basal ganglia (although surely Milton's blindness is more than merely a literary theme). They will rightly explain that *Oliver Twist* makes most sense when you understand the Reform laws but not particularly when you bring in the rise of comparative anatomy (though surely children, oppressed by child labor laws, are constructed as much by the incomplete development of brain and bone and tissue as by ideologies of childhood).

Likewise, clinicians and scientists will perhaps acknowledge that reading novels and poems might contribute to one's being a well-rounded person but probably wouldn't contribute much to the design of an experiment or help a surgeon perform a triple bypass, even if the patient happens to be an English professor (although she could point out, from a cultural perspective, that coronary artery bypass surgery did not exist before the 1960s, that it is now performed on half a million Americans annually, and that presumably very few of them are among the 16 percent of US citizens—a percentage far larger among minorities—who are not covered by health insurance).

So it would seem that C. P. Snow's lament about the two cultures—forever wedded by inverse dialectical relations but doomed to sleep in separate bedrooms—must be sadly acknowledged.

Or not.

We want to send forth a clarion call, invoke a manifesto (despite any residual modernist nostalgia) in the great tradition of the many who have believed enough in print and reading to think that setting into words a counterintuitive, radical proposition will have some larger effect on knowledge. Obviously the *Communist Manifesto*, the Port Huron Statement, and the "Cyborg Manifesto" have had some profound effects. Other manifestos have had less calculable or even negligible effects. The spirit behind a manifesto, however, is less about measurable change than it is about imagined effects and reconceived communities.

It isn't that we believe, by stringing some imperative phrases together, that we can single-handedly change the way knowledge is formed. Rather, the reality is that this transformation is already under way. In every university, in almost every department, there are already scholars working in interdisciplinary fields that require, even demand, a merger of science and society. From people working on women and health in a gender studies program to professors of English studying how psychological knowledge is used in early twentieth-century novels to disability studies graduate students concerned with the intersection of race and ability—you find a grassroots, broadly distributed group of researchers who are treading the boundaries between science and the humanities. And on the other side of the divide, you have bioethicists trying to understand how cultural values influence medical choices and medical educators trying to see how narrative can have therapeutic implications. The list of fields doing de facto biocultures is enormous. These include: public health, medical education, medical humanities, bioethics, criminal justice, epidemiology, identity and body studies, medical anthropology, medical sociology, history of medicine, philosophy of medicine, African American studies, queer studies, Asian American studies, Latino-Latina studies, and the list goes on.

So if academics and others are already voting with their research feet, why come up with complications for the head? First, there isn't a good umbrella term to describe what all these folks are doing. You can't call it bioethics, or disability studies, or science studies, or medical humanities, or anything else that won't in effect exclude a wide variety of other work. Second, by giving the name *biocultures* to these varied activities, we hope to consolidate and validate this terrain. For example, before *disability studies* became an accepted term, people working in a variety of allied fields and with a variety of impairments did not necessarily see any commonality in their varied approaches. But with the advent of an umbrella term, a new and exciting synergy has come to pass. Likewise with nanotechnology, feminist studies, and critical race theory. We are not necessarily nominalists, but we do believe in the power of a name to consolidate scattered research agendas and to generate change.

Beyond the work of specific researchers, we also need to pay attention to the broad categories of knowledge we are calling science and humanities. It wasn't always true that they were divided by a rigid firewall. In the eighteenth and early nineteenth centuries, people might do scientific work and also pursue a serious interest in literary matters. The rise of professions put an end to such hybrid interests. Part of the project of biocultures is to trace the history of that divide. We want to understand the process by which certain researchers became associated with calling their results "hard" facts and others became associated with "soft" values. While we don't deny the existence of facts, as data confirmed, for example, through a process of randomized double-blind experiments, we do question the notion that some facts are harder than others. We do question the social and discursive strategies and rules that produce the conditions for facts to arise. And we do question the notion that the humanities is a realm cut off from facts and restricted to the study of values and feelings.

In questioning the science/humanities, facts/values divide, we also believe that a better and stronger science can emerge from a productive engagement with the knowledge base developed over the past hundred years in the humanities and social sciences. This argument stresses that science is only as good as its categories and methods—and that methods and categories have been thoroughly questioned, elaborated, and refined on the humanities side of the divide. For example, many scientific studies in their protocols use race as a category. Researchers might be studying the effects of a particular drug on African Americans (as compared to its effects on the "white" population). Most experiments use a very blunt instrument in determining who is African American: simply asking the subjects, as the national census does, to self-identify. On the humanities side of the campus, however, the issue of race has been analyzed to a much more sophisticated degree than a simple notion of self-identification. Wouldn't experiments using "race" be better—produce more reliable facts—if they employed a biocultural notion of what race in fact *means*?

There are significant advantages in increasingly specialized professional subfields that can produce technological and conceptual breakthroughs by means of intensely localized analysis. Such analysis, among its side benefits, tends to spin off new interdisciplinary subfields that further advance knowledge. So this manifesto isn't a call to abolish specialization, whether in the sciences or in the humanities. And we recognize the dangers of too broad or too general a way of knowing that may dilute knowledge or excuse ignorance. (A breathtaking reductiveness is often achieved by a structural or strategic ignoring of the knowledge base of other disciplines.) To be frank, knowing what the other discourse thinks can be plain confusing. Life is so much easier if we keep to our own kind.

But knowledge isn't an easy proposition.

The biggest counterarguments in this kind of discussion inevitably involve airplanes. Science and medicine, particularly at the research end, are conflated with technological advances, and the argument goes something like this: every time you fly in an airplane, you prove that science isn't socially constructed and that science knows what it's doing. And this specious argument can be extended to the claim that literature, opera, art, and social science don't have the faintest thing to do with keeping that plane up in the air or guiding it to a destination.

In response, we'd say—keep the airplanes flying, but we have much to add about the history of aviation, representation of flight in literature, the metaphorics of being sky high, the economics of global transportation, the sociology of travel, and so on and so on. Likewise, keep the brain scans coming and keep studying how serotonin works, but we have much to say about the mind-body problem and can help interpret data; so, for example, when you are studying where OCD lives in the brain, you don't assume that OCD is a free-standing, simple disease rather than a complex set of observations and behaviors (a disease entity) linked inextricably to cultural norms.

In the end, all branches of knowledge interpret. Interpretation isn't all that they do, but it constitutes a massive common ground. Scientists set up experiments to generate data that they interpret. Literary critics interpret texts. Judges interpret the law. Sign language interpreters and translators transform one language into another. Theologians interpret the Bible or the Koran. Sociologists interpret human activity, and anthropologists interpret kinship systems and modes of behavior. Psychoanalysts interpret dreams, and neurologists interpret PET scans of dreams. If we are all interpreting data, then we are doing more or less the same thing. If we can't help interpreting, if interpretation is something that humans do across cultures, wouldn't it make sense from a biocultural perspective to consider minds as embodied, as constrained or enabled in their interpretative acts by the structure of brain and body in connection with a material environment always shaped or informed by culture? Wouldn't we all benefit by learning the rules or norms by which various discourses produce and interpret their findings? Wouldn't such knowledge help us improve our own perhaps distinctive interpretative norms and skills? Biocultures argues for a community of interpreters, across disciplines, willing to learn from each other.

This learning, while not discord free, offers a model for dialogue and holds out a promise that interpretative disagreements need not become occasions for violent conflict. It also suggests that the humanities may learn from other disciplines how to study significant textual features and affiliations accessible outside a narrow or exclusive focus on interpretation—features perhaps traceable through explorations in cognitive neuroscience such as fMRI brain imaging studies or through anthropological explorations in material culture and in social practice, which connect language and sign systems with what meaning (or meaning alone) cannot convey.

To this end, we need to change our modes of thinking, the arrangement of our discourses, the inviolability of our professions. We need to develop curricula so that we can do biocultures better. Now, at this moment, most bioculturalists are amateurs. The work they have done outside of their own field is based on curiosity, interest, and obsession. They have learned a second discipline, often with the imperfections and indelible accents that mark a second language. What we need now is a way that students in the humanities can learn how to do experiments and that students in science can learn about philosophy and theory. We need to find such a way before students have learned to speak an inherited, confining, discredited language of hard and soft, of fact and value, of mine and yours. Maybe the liberal arts never were as liberal or freeing as its proponents believed—liberal, that is, in the etymological sense that referred to a knowledge worthy of (slave-owning) citizens as distinct from slaves. Maybe what we need is even a new program or division of biocultural studies, where important questions such as what constitutes freedom cannot be divorced from equally important (and intrinsically related) scientific questions about humans and their limits.

The side benefit of a biocultural revolution is an informed citizenry. In the old days we taught civics because we recognized that ordinary citizens needed basic knowledge of their polity so they could vote intelligently and discuss reasonably in the public sphere. Now we need to teach biocultures so that ordinary citizens can understand the scientific advances (often inextricable from ethical difficulties) that will impact our lives and the lives of future citizens. Most citizens today could not reasonably vote on such issues as stem-cell research, nanotechnology, genomic and genetic screening, climate change, energy consumption, and so on—yet nothing short of the destiny of the human race and the Earth are at stake.

So what starts out as a donnish call to bring the sciences and the humanities together concludes on a millennialist (not necessarily alarmist) note. The issue isn't merely academic; in fact, the academic side of things turns out to be something far more than what the public means by the phrase "merely academic." Is it in keeping with a manifesto to claim that the outcome is necessary, historic, revolutionary, earth changing? If so, then we risk the claim. The impending risks that follow from continuing down the old science-humanities divide may make the time for renewed academic risk taking seem absolutely urgent.

This is a manifesto not only about risks but also about benefits. The benefits of a biocultural approach are many, varied, and, at this point, unpredictable. As you read, we hope that you may be moved to imagine additional possibilities within a biocultural approach. No manifesto, however, should conclude without a series of provocative assaults on the received wisdom it disputes. You may load these bullet points into your computer and fire them off to friends and foe. The specter of biocultures is upon us.

- Science and humanities are incomplete without each other.
- It is untrue that the humanities are the realm of values and the sciences the realm of facts.
- Science isn't hard, and the humanities aren't soft.
- You can't fully understand the results of a given data set without knowing the historical, social, cultural, and discursive fields surrounding the data.
- Any contemporary research needs more than a cursory background in history and in the history of the concepts it employs.
- You can't study a subject that is an object.
- You can't study an object that isn't a subject.
- Diseases are disease entities.
- If you divide truths in half you get half-truths.
- If you divide knowledge, your knowledge is divided.
- Pain is always in your head because your brain is.
- Nothing human is universal or atemporal.
- Embodiment is necessarily biological, and knowledge is always embodied.
- A fact is a socially produced conclusion.
- Bodies are always cultural and biological.
- Selves today are embodied, biologized, shaped by medical knowledge.
- The body—whose, what, when, where—is always in question.

- The boundary between organic and inorganic is no longer clear.
- Technology has become human; humans have become technologies.
- Patients and experimental subjects are part of the decision-making process.
- Science can be postmodern; postmodernisms can be scientific.
- Biology, as a science, cannot exist outside culture; culture, as a practice, cannot exist outside biology.

CHAPTER TEN

Biocultural Knowledge

Anyone with the slightest understanding of biopower might have had a moment of hesitation as well as relief when Barack Obama said: "The truth is that promoting science isn't just about providing resources—it's about protecting free and open inquiry. . . . It's about ensuring that facts and evidence are never twisted or obscured by politics or ideology. It's about listening to what our scientists have to say, even when it's inconvenient— especially when it's inconvenient. Because the highest purpose of science is the search for knowledge, truth and a greater understanding of the world around us."[1]

It is significant that Obama thinks that science should be free of the political as well as synonymous with truth and understanding. Perhaps he didn't read Foucault when I assigned it to him in the class I taught at Columbia University in 1983 when he was my student.

There has been a considerable body of knowledge on the subject of biopower and biopolitics. Obviously Michel Foucault has written most notably on this subject, indeed in some sense inventing it as an organized discourse. Surely scholars of gender and race have a prehistory of noting the intersection between bodies and power, but Foucault has laid out certain major propositions and ideas in this regard. In dialogue with Foucault have been Antonio Negri and Michael Hardt, along with Gilles Deleuze and Felix Guattari. Georgio Agamben has written about the division between *bios* and *zoe*. Many others—the list is too long—have explored these various intersections.

So what does the idea of biocultures add to biopower and biopolitics? Why not just stick with those rather powerful and suggestive terms? I am using *biocultures* to add a concept beyond what Hardt and Negri call "immaterial labor," by which they mean modes of communication through media, the Internet, and so on. Discussions of biopower tend to think of culture, if they talk about it, as a technical formation or a form of verbal or digital discourse. Michel Foucault in an interview said that any one of his few references to the literary in his work is "the object of a report, not part of an analysis. . . . It was a point of rest, a halt"; he says that he uses literature in a negative sense. "excluding it."[2] I am asserting that biopower would do well with a stronger claim to culture, art, literature, film and so on, as something more along the lines of symbolic production, but with a greater sense of it in the public and social sphere. I am thinking of what we might want to call biocultural studies.

We might want to consider Agamben's severing of *zoe* from *bios*, a move that institutes the sovereign exception, the foundation of government. If you separate bare life from civil life, you have created the foundation for biopower. Foucault also uses a notion of separation to found modernity, the separation of disciplinary discourses from discourses of biopower, and Deleuze notes these act of separating as really an act of "folding." But instantiating separations can be risky business, particularly when you don't see your own discipline as part of some kind of partly heuristic and partly power-driven motive. What concerns me is the way that certain separations or foldings have been either made or ignored. In talking about power and politics it has been too often easy to exclude culture or to see culture as either the handmaiden of power and/or the site of resistance to that power. In either case, culture is peripheral and marginal, aleatory.

While studies in biopower focus on the split between discipline, with its thanatopolitics, and modernity, with its biopower, they often fail to see that the very terms used in thinking about culture and power are misleading since they seem to place culture as a function of power, at a second remove from the authority and force of power.

That move to divide, I would argue, comes about from the primal separation or rupture that happened concurrently with the historical rise of biopower in the nineteenth century. That is the division between science and the humanities. We can trace a genealogy of this division, which I cannot do here but to which I want to refer. Scientists (and the word was invented in the 1840s as a kind of a reverse synonym to the word *artist*) were initially deemed people with an interest in nature, not credentialed researchers—as the scientist was not expected to be uniquely separate from practitioners of art and culture. But the history of the concept over the following fifty years is one in which the ideological claim becomes increasingly accepted that scientists deal in a very concrete and provable kind of truth while artists, humanists, novelists, critics, and so on deal in something far more impressionistic, in less accountable forms of knowing. This claim is buttressed by something called "the scientific method"—although no one has ever been able to say exactly what this is, and it is clear looking at the origin of the concept in the mid-nineteenth century that "the" scientific method could be used in many areas of scholarship, including the humanities. It would be more accurate to say that an experimental method came to be seen as foundational for science, although science certainly included much that was not experimental. In the mid-nineteenth century J. A. Froude, for example, wrote: "Neither history, nor any other knowledge, could be obtained except by scientific methods."[3]

If we try to get a snapshot of the moment in which science attempted to claim this authority, we get a very interesting set of observations. In the following, I will be looking a bit more closely at the late nineteenth-century naturalist John Burroughs's essay "Science and Literature." In it Burroughs notes the beginning of this split—"the distrust" between science and literature—and cites Huxley as one who "taunts the poets with sensual caterwauling" and the poets as those who "taunt the professor and his ilk with gross materialism." Burroughs goes on to observe, "Science is founding schools and colleges from which the study of literature, as such, is to be excluded; and it is becoming clamorous for the positions occupied by the classics in the curriculum."[4]

We can observe the beginning of this folding, in which either category can only arise by excluding the other, but as with all foldings, the exterior is brought inside the new construct. For science, the human, in the form of the humanities, had to be excluded by including its value, its truth claims. Science was thus not the study of mere things but, as Obama now says, of truth.

Science is seen as "democratic, its aims and methods in keeping with the great modern movement; while literature is alleged be to aristocratic in its spirit and tendencies. Literature is for the few, science is for the many."[5] What is fascinating in this on-the spot observation is the notion that science is democratic, that anyone can learn it and master its insights, while literature takes time and leisure to accumulate the body of knowledge required for understanding and judgment. Science is seen as entrepreneurially colonizing the university and making its claim to better kinds of knowledge.

Burroughs makes the counterargument, as did others, like Wilkie Collins in his insightful novel *Heart and Science:* that science is inhuman and technical, while literature is the place of emotions and lived truth. That argument gets picked up in fiction with the character of the mad scientist who does things that endanger humanity in the quest for knowledge, as illustrated beginning with Dr. Frankenstein and moving through Dr. Moreau.

In that move to claim feelings and values, humanists sealed their fate and collaborated in the great discursive divide between science and the humanities. Science could then make the argument that understanding *zoe* and *techne* could produce a kind of bioknowledge that trumped the kinds of bioknowledge produced by understanding *bios* and culture. And largely cultural critics acceded to this notion by developing quasi-romantic notions of the role and value of their knowledges. Burroughs cites Wordsworth's "the world is too much with us late and soon" as a work that "intimated that our science . . . has put us 'out of tune' with nature." And he approvingly notes that Goethe says, "Microscopes and telescopes, properly considered, put our human eyes out of their natural, healthy, and profitable point of view." Burroughs's gloss on this quote is that Goethe "probably meant that artificial knowledge obtained by the aid of instruments, and therefore by a kind of violence and inquisition, a kind of dissecting and dislocating process, is less innocent, is less sweet and wholesome, than natural knowledge, the fruits of our natural faculties and perceptions."[6] His reference to "violence" and "dissecting" signals to the nineteenth-century reader a reference to the antivivisection movement, which was instrumental in fostering a rift between humanists, who valued the lives of dogs, cats, and horses, and scientists, whose cruel dissections were performed without anesthesia and often in public, defending themselves with the claims of truth and utility. Opting for a variety of vitalism and essentialism, writers like Burroughs ended up making the humanities religious and the sciences godless, the former human and the latter aiming for divine knowledge through purely technical means.

Burroughs, however, does acknowledge that even his division is artificial, and I want to blame both humanists and scientists—what a ridiculous set of binaries—for creating the situation we face today. He cites Goethe, Darwin, Audubon, and Von Humboldt as examples of scientists and humanists who cross over through their interest and sympathies with nature: "If Audubon had not felt other than a scientific interest in the birds— namely a human interest, an interest born of sentiment—would he ever have written their biographies as he did?" Of Darwin: "All his works have a human and almost poetic side." Of Von Humboldt: "The noble character, the poetic soul, shines out in all his works and gives them a value above and beyond their scientific worth."[7]

What writers like Burroughs fail to see or appreciate is that throwing in the towel on this issue—rendering unto science the right to distinct and provable kinds of knowledge—created the rise of incomplete knowledges, partial knowledges whose claims to totality are based on partial understanding—what I might call demi-knowledges.

At the end of his essay Burroughs does acknowledge the value of science as "tending to foster a disinterested love of truth . . . stimulating the desire to see and know things as they really are."[8] It doesn't take a literary sleuth to see that he is paraphrasing Mathew Arnold. Arnold's notion of criticism is in the same sense scientific, with its cold hard flame of disinterested observation. In an amusing and allegorical finale Burroughs imagines a scene in which the true poet and the true scientist take a walk in nature "not estranged" from each other. The scientist is younger and "more active and inquiring," seeing the individual parts of nature, while the poet is older and has "more an air of leisurely contemplation and enjoyment," seeing the virtues of the whole: "The interests of the two in the universe are widely different, yet in no true sense are they hostile or mutually destructive."[9] Burroughs wants to reconcile what had become a rift in nineteenth-century society. This vision of the lion of science lying down with the lamb of poetry ends the essay but is not a resolution so much as a fantasy. The division itself is destructive to both branches of knowledge because it makes one the dominant discourse of power and the other the ancillary, anaclitic handmaiden. Like Hegel's master and slave, the two are now interdependent, based on various claims and renunciations, but are largely unaware of the deal they have made in the process of instantiating the demi-knowing of each of their discourses.

Obviously the missing figures in the reconciling of the humanities and science in Burroughs's account are Marx and Freud, a list to which I would add Zola—all three considered themselves humanists and scientists. Indeed, Marx defined what he did as historical materialism, which Marx saw as *wissenschaft*, that is, as a science. The three did not accept the division between science and lesser forms of knowledge, claiming the brand name of *science*—whose linguistic root after all just means knowledge—without subjecting it to the criteria demanded by scientists—that is, to a demand for experimentation. Indeed, Zola regarded his novels as experiments.

The idea that experimentation will yield a better kind of knowledge than simply hypothesis and observation is, at the end of the workday, a very limited argument. It depends on notions that peer review and repetition can guarantee absolute knowledge, and it leaves out, of course, the notion that any data set must be interpreted in order to enter the archive of scientific knowledge. Nineteenth-century criteria for experimentation would seem quite impressionistic by our contemporary standards. And perhaps most telling, its deep unconscious, the exterior folded within, must deny that truth can come in any other form. Freud and Marx were observers and deducers; Zola believed that literature could be case history and that the mixing of genetic characters could yield experimental results. The point is that the choice did not have to be between science and culture—the false choice presented both by both "sides"; rather, the choice was between complete and incomplete knowledges.

To return to biopower and biocultures, I hope I have shown, if only provisionally, that any genealogy of knowledge that fails to acknowledge the role of culture in the development of biopower will be incomplete. And by *culture* I don't mean only the way that biopower acts in the world through symbolic production, but rather the way that histories of knowing have largely precluded discussions of their own coming into being—the genealogy and operation of their own culture—especially the separation of culture from science, which produced the current crisis of knowledge.

But *is* there a crisis of knowledge? I would argue that the need for a biocultural understanding of our moment is more pressing than ever, and here I will now bring in the topic of education. In order to be a citizen now it is necessary to have certain kinds of knowledge to participate effectively in the public sphere and the political sphere. With controversies over the environment, the biosphere, stem-cell research, the role of gender and transgender, race, health care, abortion, pandemics, droughts and famine, disabilities, and so on, there is a necessity for complex understandings of the way that science impacts society. To be a student or scholar in the humanities, it is also increasingly necessary to have biocultural knowledges. That means that we as teachers and our students need to be aware that we can't function fully if we only know one half of the humanities/science division.

How can we do our work on race, gender, politics, disability, and identity in general without recourse to this biocultural knowledge? How can we discuss character in novels and drama without recourse to understanding the human mind and affect? How can we teach the literature of an era without knowing what types of biocultural knowledge was available to, say, the groundlings in the Globe or the readers of Dickens's fascicules? What did Faulkner and his readers know about people with cognitive disabilities? How did eugenic thought affect writers like Dreiser and Faulkner? What did the Marquis de Sade know about medicine and surgery? How much did discussions around neurasthenia and monomania become part of the narratives of Melville, Poe, and Dostoyevsky? Or for that matter, how much has the *DSM* affected the writing of contemporary authors? Apparently early silent film actors and even the dancers at the Moulin Rouge at the turn of the twentieth century found themselves moving according the way hysterics described by Charcot did.

I list all this not to say that as researchers and educated citizens we need to know science, because that itself would simply repeat the science/humanities binary. And my call isn't so much to say "let's all get together and do this" as it is to signal that this work is well under way—and that it has come about by necessity as language studies has become cultural studies, which has become biocultural studies.

I hope that, if anything, this book has shown that in the twenty-first century we can no longer afford to be without a biocultural way of knowing. Identity in our time is in fact biocultural identity. To paraphrase Socrates, we might say "Know thy biocultural self."

Notes

Preface

1. I am professor of English in the College of Arts and Sciences, professor of disability and human development in the College of Applied Health Sciences, and professor of medical education in the College of Medicine.

Chapter 1

1 Lennard J. Davis, *Enforcing Normalcy: Disability, Deafness, and the Body* (New York and London: Verso, 1995), chapter 1.

2. See Walter Benn Michaels, *The Trouble with Diversity: How We Learned to Love Diversity and Ignore Inequality* (New York: Metropolitan Books, 2006), for more on the relationship of diversity to neoliberalism.

3. I don't have the space to elaborate this point here, but neoliberal advertising stresses the idea of belonging to a niche group rather than the quality, superiority, or price of the thing to be consumed. Pepsi originated this type of advertising based on lifestyle in the early 1960s, overturning its older ad, which stressed size and lower price (compared to Coke). The phrase "the Pepsi Generation" used in the ad implied that if you drank their product, you would be associated with youth and vigor. Our current advertising is designed to appeal to niche markets (many diverse markets) and to suggest that using an Apple product will associate you with a cohort made up of people who believe what you believe. In contrast, for example, Roland Barthes's analysis of the semiology of advertising (which he did before lifestyle ads became in vogue) suggests that either effectiveness or nationality was important in soap ads and in pasta commercials. The "italianness" of the product didn't make the eater more Italian; it suggested that Italians know better than anyone how to make pasta and that as a French person you might want to eat products that can best suggest "italianness." In short, old-style capitalism wanted to suggest you buy its product because it was the best or most affordable one; neocapitalism suggests you'd like to be part of a particular diverse group, and consuming a product might help you do that.

4. Will Kymlicka, *Multicultural Citizenship* (Oxford: Oxford University Press, 1995), 121.

5. Manfred B. Steger and Ravi K. Roy, *Neoliberalism: A Very Short Introduction* (Oxford: Oxford University Press, 2010), 11.

6. Steger and Roy, *Neoliberalism*, 53.

7. Georgio Agamben, *Homo Sacer: Sovereign Power and Bare Life*, trans. Daniel Heller-Roazen (Stanford: Stanford University Press, 1998).

8. However, a new trend in posthuman thought, expressed by Stacy Alaimo, Jasbir Puar, Theresa de Lauretis, and Victoria Pitts-Taylor, among others, suggests that feminists and Foucauldians, for example, have erred in one direction by stressing the totally constructed nature of the body. They point to a return to the body, its materiality, as a recuperative corrective, although they don't wish to be naïve about that materiality.

9. For more on this subject, see Dorothy Roberts, *Fatal Invention: How Science, Politics, and Big Business Re-create Race in the Twenty-First Century* (New York: New Press, 2011).

10. Victoria Pitts-Taylor, *Surgery Junkies: Wellness and Pathology in Cosmetic Culture* (New Jersey: Rutgers University Press, 2007.

11. Lennard J. Davis and David Morris, "The Biocultures Manifesto," originally published in *New Literary History*, appearing in this volume as chapter 9.

12. See Gilles Deleuze and Felix Guattari, *Nomads*; Jasbir Puar, *Terrorist Assemblages: Homonationalism in Queer Times* (Chapel Hill: Duke University Press, 2007).

13. Eva Kittay points out in a yet unpublished paper that normal may not always be good, as when an older person has the blood pressure of a twenty-year-old. This is true, but that kind of outcome is still normal in the sense of good and healthy.

14. See the Icarus Project: Navigating the Space Between Brilliance and Madness at http://www.theicarusproject.net

15. Except in the case of "wannabes" or what some people call "transability." Those who fit into this category want to be disabled, although they are not, and so might either choose to amputate limbs or choose to live in the manner of a disabled person. The point is that this is a lifestyle choice that fits nicely into the neoliberal paradigm for diverse bodies I've articulated.

16. Giorgio Agamben, *State of Exception*, trans. Kevin Attell (Chicago: University of Chicago Press, 2005), 40.

17. Agamben, *State of Exception*, 40.

18. Michael A. Peters, *Poststructuralism, Marxism, and Neoliberalism: Between Theory and Politics* (Lanham, MD: Rowman and Littlefield, 2001), 124.

19. I am not speaking here of the obvious fact that all identities have an element of unfreedom in the sense that circulating cultural representations will pigeonhole anyone into the generally accepted stereotypes of any identity. One can therefore choose any identity, but the interpretation and signification of that identity will be socially determined.

20. It is interesting too that the central rationale of the proabortion movement is that a woman has a "right to choose." Rather than couching the discussion in moral or ethical considerations, the shorthand and fully understandable reason given is that the central right is choice, which trumps all other arguments.

21. Walter Benn Michaels points out that no one is arguing for poverty as a diversity category. No claim is made that we need to maintain poverty culture.

22. We do not publicly refer to disabled people as *zoe* anymore, but we should remember that disabled people were the first to go to the gas chambers, before homosexuals, Jews, Gypsies, and other groups. The logic for the disabled as *zoe* is a deep part of global history—including the institutionalization of people with disabilities, their sterilization, and now the use of brain implants almost exclusively in affectively disabled people (deep-stem brain stimulation) and Deaf people (cochlear implants).

Chapter 2

1. James Boswell, *Life of Johnson* (London: Oxford University Press, 1904; rpt., 1965), 333.

2. Lennard J. Davis, "The End of Identity Politics and the Beginning of Dismodernism: On Disability as an Unstable Category," in Lennard J. Davis, *Bending Over Backwards: Disability, Dismodernism, and Other Difficult Positions* (New York: New York University Press, 2002), 8–32.

3. Carlos Clark Drazen, who was working on her dissertation with me before her untimely death, was intent on proving in that work that the analogy between disability and minority identity was the wrong one. While understanding how the disability movement had modeled itself on the civil rights movement, her dissertation aimed to prove that a better analogy was between disability status and immigrant or displaced person identity.

4. Greg Bishop, "In a Softball Case, a Thorny Debate Over Who Qualifies as Gay," *New York Times*, June 30, 2011.

5. Suzanna Denuta Walters, guest blog, "Born This Way," *Chronicle of Higher Education*, July 6, 2011, http://chronicle.com/blogs/brainstorm/born-this-way/37016.

6. Carrie Sandahl, "Blind Man: Disability Identity Politics and Performance Author(s)," *Theatre Journal* 56, no. 4, (Dec. 2004): 582, 583.

7. See my essay "Dangerous Ideas," *Chronicle of Higher Education*, June 12, 2011, http://chronicle.com/article/Dangerous-Ideas/127790/.

8. See http://books.google.com/ngrams/graph?content=postpositivist+realism&year_start=1990&year_end=2008&corpus=0&smoothing=3. I don't use Ngram with any sense that it provides certainty, just for illustrative and rhetorical purposes. Accessed 5/20/2013.

9. Stanley Fish, "Sokal's Bad Joke," *New York Times*, May 21, 1996, http://physics.nyu.edu/sokal/fish.html.

10. Tobin Siebers, *Disability Theory* (Ann Arbor: University of Michigan Press, 2008), 60.

11. Siebers, *Disability Theory*, 67.

12. Siebers, *Disability Theory*, 67.

13. Siebers, *Disability Theory*, 67.

14. David Morris, *Culture of Pain* (Berkeley: University of California, 1993) and Ronald Schleifer, *Pain and Suffering* (New York: Routledge, 2013).

15. Siebers, *Disability Theory*, 67.
16. Siebers, *Disability Theory*, 68.
17. Siebers, *Disability Theory*, 81.
18. Siebers, *Disability Theory*, 70.
19. Siebers, *Disability Theory*, 83.
20. Siebers, *Disability Theory*, 83.
21. Anne Mollow, "Identity Politics and Disability Studies: A Critique of Recent Theory," *Michigan Quarterly Review* (Spring 2004): 269–96.
22. Peter Singer, *Animal Liberation: A New Ethics for Our Treatment of Animals* (New York: Random House, 1975); *Practical Ethics* (Cambridge: Cambridge University Press, 1979).
23. Sunaura Taylor, "Humane Meat? No Such Thing," *Yes*, March 27, 2011.
24. Giorgio Agamben, *Homo Sacer: Sovereign Power and Bare Life* , trans. Daniel Heller-Roazen (Palo Alto, CA:Stanford University Press, 1995).
25. John Kristeva, *Powers of Horror: An Essay on Abjection* (New York: Columbia University, 1982).

Chapter 3

1. Kate Murphy, "Turning Every Stone for a Perfect Fit, *New York Times*, Dec. 24, 2009, http://www.nytimes.com/2009/12/24/garden/24mosaic.html?page wanted=all.
2. Lennard Davis, "Let Actors with Disabilities Play Characters with Disabilities," *Huffington Post*, December 7, 2009. http://www.huffingtonpost.com/lennard-davis/let-actors-with-disabilit_b_380266.html.
3. Daniel Holloway, "GLAAD: Only 6 Disabled Primetime Characters," *Hollywood Reporter*, 10/6/2010, http://www.hollywoodreporter.com/news/glaad-only-6-disabled-primetime-15312.
4. "Controversy behind Eastwood's 'Invictus,'" December 11, 2009. http://www.pri.org/arts-entertainment/movies/clint-eastwood-invictus1771.html.
5. Jewish characters are rarely played by Jewish actors. See "11 Best Jewish Movie Characters Played by Non-Jewish Actors," www.11points.com/movies/11_Best_Jewish_Movie_Characters_Played_by_Non_Jewish_Actors, accessed August 15, 2013.
6. Rosemarie Garland-Thomson, "Hot Sex and Disability at the Movies," *Huffington Post Blog*, 2/21/2013.

Chapter 4

1. See http://www.mental-health-today.com/dep/dsm.htm.
2. Peter Kramer, *Against Depression* (New York: Penguin, 2005), Kindle location 2608.
3. See Gary Greenberg, *Manufacturing Depression: The Secret History of a Modern Disease* (New York: Simon and Schuster, 2010); Allan V. Horowitz and Jerome Wakefield, *The Loss of Sadness: How Psychiatry Transformed Normal Sorrow into Depressive Disorder* (New York: Oxford University Press, 2007); David Healy, *The Anti-Depressant Era* (Cambridge: Harvard University Press, 1997); Robert Whitaker,

Anatomy of an Epidemic: Magic Bullets, Psychiatric Drugs, and the Astonishing Rise of Mental Illness in America (New York: Broadway, 2011); Irving Kirst, *The Emperor's New Drugs: Exploding the Antidepressant Myth* (New York: Basic, 2010); Joanna Montcrief, *The Myth of the Chemical Cure: A Critique of Psychiatric Drug Treatment* (London: Palgrave, 2009); among others.

4. See Herb Jutchins and Stuart A. Kirk, *Making Us Crazy: DSM, the Psychiatric Bible and the Creation of Mental Disorders;* Peter Conrad, *The Medicalization of Society: On the Transformation of Human Conditions into Treatable Disorders;* for example.

5. It's not entirely clear that Jefferson meant "happiness" in the sense we use it today. Some speculate that his use was based on Locke's "life, liberty, and property." Others think he might have found the phrase in Dr. Johnson's work, others that the use of the word traces back to Epicurus and refers to civic happiness, which relates to civic virtue.

6. Healy, *Anti-Depressant Era.*

7. Frank J. Ayd Jr., *Recognizing the Depressed Patient* (New York: Grune and Stratton, 1961).

8. Ayd, *Recognizing the Depressed Patient*, v.

9. How can I smile
When love don't seem worthwhile?
I'm left with the blues in my heart.

How can I live?
What is there life can give
As long as we're apart?

How can I go on
Knowing that you are gone?
I'm left with the blues in my heart.

10. My heart is heavy as lead
Because the blues has done spread
Rocks in my bed.

All night long I weep
So how can I sleep
with rocks in my bed.

11. But there is one thing I know
A man's a two-face, a worrisome thing
Who'll leave ya to sing the blues in the night
Yes the lonely, lonely blues in the night

12. The brook runs into the river, river runs into the sea
If I don't run into my baby, a train is goin' to run into me.

13. R. C. Kessler et. al, "Lifetime and 12-Month prevalence of DSM-III-R Psychiatric Disorders in the United States,: *Archive of General Psychiatry* 51, nos. 8–19 (1994): .

14. H. G. Ruhé, N. S. Mason, and Aart H. Schene, "Mood Is Indirectly Related to Serotonin, Norepinephrine and Dopamine Levels in Humans: A Meta-Analysis of Monoamine Depletion Studies,: *Molecular Psychiatry* 12 (2007): 331–59, cited in Irving Kirsch, *The Emperor's New Drugs: Exploding the Antidepressant Myth*, 92.

15. Jeffrey R Lacasse and Jonathan Leo, "Serotonin and Depression: A Disconnect between the Advertisements and the Scientific Literature," *PloS Medicine* 2, no. 12 (2005): http://www.ncbi.nlm.nih.gov/pmc/articles/PMC1277931/.

16. J. Radden, ed., *The Nature of Melancholy from Aristotle to Kristeva* (New York: Oxford University Press, 2000), 55–60.

17. http://www.democraticunderground.com/1255389. This link includes the ad mentioned and others of a similar vein from the same period depicting depressed or anxious women in domestic settings.

18. The latest draft of the forthcoming *DSM V* recommends that the bereavement exception be shortened to a month from two months.

19. Interestingly, such use of drugs coincided with the criminalization of opiates, which resulted from Prohibition. As alcohol was made difficult to get, many people switched to marijuana, barbiturates, amphetamines, and other drugs. One could make the case that the criminalization and restriction of opiates, widely used earlier in common patent remedies like gripe water for babies, created a special class of professionals who could prescribe such medicines, and therefore doctors came to be seen as soothers of psychic distress. When one could go to the local pharmacy and self-soothe, the physician was not necessarily needed.

20. Greenberg, *Manufacturing Depression*, 179.

21. A good account of this suppression is found in Irving Kirsch's *Emperor's New Drugs*. Kirsch was able to obtain these suppressed trials under the Freedom of Information Act. See pp. 23–54.

22. Kirsch, *Emperor's New Drugs*, 4.

23. Kramer, *Against Depression*, 325–34.

24. Kirsch, *Emperor's New Drugs*, 100.

25. David Healy in *Pharmageddon* argues that clinical trials are actually a very bad idea since it is quite easy to manipulate data, and then once the trial has been accepted as true, it is very hard to undo the damage it may have done.

26. Kramer, *Against Depression*, location 2368.

27. J. McKinley, "Get That Man Some Prozac," *New York Times*, Feb. 28, 1999, http://www.who.int/mental_health/management/depression/definition/en/.

28. Lennard J. Davis, *Enforcing Normalcy: Disability, Deafness, and the Body* (New York: Verso, 1995).

29. Alan Horowitz and Jerome C. Wakefield, *The Loss of Sadness: How Psychiatry Transformed Normal Sorrow Into Depression* (New York: Oxford University Press, 2007).

30. Horowitz and Wakefield, *Loss of Sadness*, 50–52.

31. Perhaps it is not so accepting that it celebrates depression. Abby Wilkinson notes that there is no equivalent to "gay pride" that could be called "mope pride." See "Slipping," in David Halperin and Valerie Traub, eds., *Gay Shame* (Chicago: University of Chicago Press, 2009), 191.

32. Ironically, the current drug named Soma, generically called Carisoprodol, is actually the drug Miltown, used in the 1960s as one of the major antianxiety and antidepressant drugs.

33. Joanna Moncrieff, *The Myth of the Chemical Cure: A Critique of Psychiatric Drug Treatment* (New York: Palgrave Macmillan, 2009), 172–73.

34. Moncrieff, *Myth of the Chemical Cure*, 173.

35. Jonathan Metzl, *Prozac on the Couch: Prescribing Gender in the Era of Wonder Drugs* (Durham, N.C.: Duke University Press, 2003),

36. Jonathan Metzl, *Prozac on the Couch.*

37. http://theicarusproject.net.

38. http://www.mindfreedom.org

39. Kay Redfield Jamison, *An Unquiet Mind,* 220.

40. Kirsch, *Emperor's New Drugs,* 3.

41. Gretchen Reynolds, "Prescribing Exercise to Treat Depression," *New York Times,* Aug. 31, 2011, http://well.blogs.nytimes.com/2011/08/31/prescribing-exercise-to-treat-depression/?ref=health.

42. Kirsch, *Emperor's New Drugs,* 150–76.

Chapter 5

1. In saying "out-of-boundary," I am committing a kind of heresy against biocultural analysis, which is premised on having nonspecialists and not medical scientists analyze researchers' data and findings. Specialists cannot or have not to any great extent engaged in a rigorous self-critique of their own basic systems.

2. An interesting question that has been raised by microtechnology is the possibility that prosthetic devices can be better than original body parts. How will super hearing aids, infrared contact lenses, more nimble and durable limbs, and super genes alter our notions of the prosthetic?

3. Nicholas Wade, "Gene Study Identifies Five Main Human Population," *New York Times,* Dec. 20, 2002. This article was based on Noah A. Rosenberg, Jonathan K. Pritchard, James L. Weber, Howard M. Cann, Kenneth K. Kidd, Lev A. Zhivotovsky, and Marcus W. Feldman, "Genetic Structure of Human Populations," *Science* 298 (2002): 2381–85.

4. Gina Kolata, "Using Genetic Tests, Ashkenazi Jews Vanquish a Disease," *New York Times,* Feb. 18, 2003.

5. Charcot, for example, said that "nervous illness of all types are innumerably more frequent among Jews than among other groups." Quoted in Sander Gilman, *Difference and Pathology: Stereotypes of Sexuality, Race and Madness* (Ithaca: Cornell University Press, 1985), 155.

6. Alcon Laboratories, "New Prostaglandin Shows Significant Reductions in 10P and Greater Effectiveness in Black Patients," press release, Mar. 20, 2001.

7. http://www.nitromed.com/pnt/about_bidil.php (accessed Dec. 31, 2012).

8. Jonathan D. Kahn, "How a Drug Becomes 'Ethnic': Law, Commerce, and the Production of Racial Categories in Medicine," *Yale Journal of Health Policy, Law and Ethics* 4 (2004): 1–46.

9. Kahn, "How a Drug Becomes 'Ethnic.'"

10. B. Smedley, A. Stith, and A. Nelson, eds., *Unequal Treatment: Confronting Racial and Ethnic Disparities in Health Care* (Washington, DC: National Academic Press, 2003).

11. N. Kriegere and S. Sidney, "Racial Discrimination and Blood Pressure: The CARDIA Study of Young Black and White Adults," *American Journal of Public Health* 86 (1996): 1370–78.

12. Troy Duster, "Buried Alive: The Concept of Race in Science," *Chronicle of*

Higher Education, Sept. 14, 2001, http://chronicle.com/weekly/v48/103/03b01101.htm

Chapter 6

1. Anne Fausto-Sterling, "The Bare Bones of Sex: Sex and Gender" in M. Wyer, M. Barbercheck, D. Giesman, H. Örün Öztürk, and M. Wayne, eds, *Women, Science, and Technology: A Reader in Feminist Science Studies* (New York: Routledge, 2001), 219–36.

2. Cultural and social factors are important in any diagnosis, and within medical practice there are fads and trends in all areas. Recently I gave a version of this talk to fourth-year medical students at Albert Einstein College of Medicine in New York. One student pointed out to me that such factors impinged on something as simple as infantile digestion, with a huge increase recently in giving infants medication for reflux. The student maintained that about one-third of all babies now in the institution where she worked were on such medication.

3. American Psychiatric Association. *Diagnostic and Statistical Manual of Mental Disorders: DSM-IV-TR* (APA, 2000).

4. I put "mentally ill" in scare quotes because there is a fundamental question, not answerable in this essay, about the ontological nature of psychic distress. Is it a disease, a condition, a philosophical problem, etc.? The history of psychiatry leads us to an understanding of why mental conditions were considered "diseases" or "illnesses," but a large body of work and many new organizations now question the disease categorization.

5. Comorbidity is a wiggle-room concept, like the cosmological constant that Einstein added to his general theory of relativity to try to keep a stationary model of the universe. Comorbidity allows for a diagnosis in the presence of extraneous symptoms. Much more needs to be analyzed in this area, but the brevity of this essay won't allow further discussion.

6. *DSM IV TR*, xxiii.

7. Robert Burton has written about the difficulty of arriving at certainty as a physician. He notes that "we aren't reliable assessors" and that physicians make "an attempt to base our opinions on as thorough a scientific understanding as possible, while simultaneously reminding ourselves and our patients that our information will necessarily have been filtered through our own personal biases, affecting our selection of evidence and even which articles trigger a sense of correctness. Once we've made this admission, we have stepped off the pedestal of certainty and into the more realistic world of likelihoods and probabilities," Robert Burton, *On Being Certain: Believing You Are Right Even When You Are Not* (New York: St. Martin, 2009), 172–73.

8. Even the *DSM's* recommendation that obsessive thinking might have a different kind of treatment from checking and ordering behaviors is a tacit admission that two different kinds of activities have been agglutinated into one disease entity. For more on OCD see my *Obsession: A History* (Chicago: University of Chicago Press, 2009).

9. "98% of Babies Manic Depressive," *Onion,* Mar. 23, 2009.

10. Some studies indicate that diagnosis of mental disorders coordinates only very slightly with reliable treatment outcomes. See, e.g., S. Kirk and H. Kutchins, "The Myth of the Reliability of DSM," *Journal of Mind and Behavior* 15 (1994): 71–86; and, more generally.

11. David Morris, *The Culture of Pain* (Berkeley: University of California Press, 1991).

12. Morris, *Culture of Pain*, 1.

13. In English one "has" a symptom. Why does one *have* it? Is it an object to have? More properly it might be said that the symptom has the person, transforming them into a patient by that having.

14. Indeed, his problem stems from his having walked from Sparta to Thebes, where on the road he meets his father and kills him. His father is on a chariot, not walking, and that murder leads to Oedipus's encounter with the Sphinx and his marrying of his mother.

15. Ludvig Wittgenstein, *On Certainty* (London: Blackwell. 1991), 3, 6e.

16. Wittgenstein, *On Certainty*, 64.

17. Davis, *Obsession*.

18. L. Aron. *A Meeting of Minds: Mutuality in Psychoanalysis* (New Jersey: Analytic Press, 1996). Stephen A. Mitchell, *Relational Concepts in Psychoanalysis* (Cambridge, Mass.: Harvard University Press, 1988).

19. Aron, *Meeting of Minds*, 149.

20. For more on hysteria see Elaine Showalter, *The Female Malady: Women, Madness, and English Culture, 1830–1980* (New York: Pantheon Books, 1985); and Juliette Mitchell, *Mad Men and Medusas: Reclaiming Hysteria* (New York: Basic Books, 2001).

21. Slavoj Zizek, *Interrogating the Real* (New York: Continuum, 2005), 316.

22. Simon Critchley, *Ethics-Politics-Subjectivity: Essays on Derrida, Levinas, and Contemporary French Thought* (London: Verso, 1999), 275.

23. Zizek, *Interrogating the Real*, 316.

Chapter 7

1. I'm using the acronym PAS for convenience, although I know it is used also to indicate "personal assistance services."

2. www.autonomynow.org.

3. The academic organization the Society for Disability Studies (SDS) joined the amicus brief against PAS without an extended discussion or vote by its general membership, as would be required in, for example, the Modern Language Association or the American Anthropological Association. In my opinion the organization abrogated its academic responsibility to examine issues and foster discussion. The subsequent remediation of this oversight by SDS's withdrawal from the amicus brief, after protest by some of its members, marked a valuable corrective to a pell-mell rush to judgment without all the information.

4. http://public.health.oregon.gov/ProviderPartnerResources/EvaluationResearch/DeathwithDignityAct/Pages/index.aspx.

5. Barbara Coombs Lee, "A Model That Integrates Assisted Dying with Excel-

lent End-of-Life Care," in Timothy E. Quill and Margaret P. Battin, eds., *Physician-Assisted Dying: The Case for Palliative Care and Patient Choice* (Baltimore: Johns Hopkins University Press, 2004), 190–202.

6. Marilyn Golden, www.dredf.org.

7. Herbert Hendin, "The Dutch Experience," in Kathleen Foley and Herbert Hendin, eds., *The Case against Assisted Suicide: For the Right to End-of-Life Care* (Baltimore: Johns Hopkins University Press, 2002), 97–121.

8. Van Delden, Visser, and Borst-Eilers, "Thirty Years' Experience with Euthanasia in the Netherlands," in Quill and Battin, *Physician-Assisted Dying*, 206.

9. Hendin, "Dutch Experience," 103.

10. George K. Kimsma and Evert Van Leeuwen, "The Netherlands: Physicians at the Bedside," in Quill and Battin, *Physician-Assisted Dying*, 222.

11. Kimmsa and Van Leeuwen, "Netherlands," 222.

12. Van der Heide, Deliens, Faisst, Nilstun, Norup, Paci, van der Wal, van der Maas, and EURELD Consortium, "End-of-Life Decision-Making in Six European Countries: Descriptive Study," *Lancet* 362 (2003): 345–50.

13. See the National Right to Life organization website: http://www.right-to-life.org/Quotes%20Archive.htm.

14. Thomas Szazs's book *Fatal Freedom* makes a strong argument for suicide in general, positing that suicide prevention is just an extension of the medicalization of life choices. Szazs contends that people like Hendin use psychiatry to brand all people who want to kill themselves as either clinically depressed or mentally ill—neither of which he believes is the case.

15. http://www.afsp.org/whats-new/bioethics_text.htm.

16. Palliative care is generally measured by the number of hospice programs a country might have. Since health care is universal in the Netherlands, most patients have long-term relations with their doctors, and the majority of people die at home. Because of that scenario, the Netherlands rated low on palliative care. In the past ten years, however, the number of hospices has increased dramatically as a result of the national debate over PAS and euthanasia.

17. Van Delden, Visser, and Borst-Eilers, "Thirty Years' Experience with Euthanasia," 207.

18. Christakis and Iwashyna, *Archives of Internal Medicine* 158 (Nov. 23, 1998): 2389–95.

19. Linda Ganzini, "The Oregon Experience," in Quill and Battin, *Physician-Assisted Dying*, 174. Also it might be worth noting that drugs like Prozac are actually not very effective in treating depression (see chap. 3).

Chapter 8

1. Lynn Gamwell and Mark Solms, *From Neurology to Psychoanalysis: Sigmund Freud's Neurological Drawings and Diagrams of the Mind* (Binghamptom: Binghamptom University Art Museum, 2006), 23.

2. Sander Gilman, *Freud, Race, and Gender* (Princeton, N.J.: Princeton University Press, 1993), 74ff

3. Sarah Franklin, *Embodied Progress: A Cultural Account of Assisted Conception* (London: Routledge, 1997), 55

4. James Strachey, *The Standard Edition of the Complete Psychological Works of Sigmund Freud*, trans. James Strachey (London: Hogarth Press, 1966), 19: 33n.

5. Strachey, *Standard Edition*, 7: 220.

6. Strachey, *Standard Edition*, 22: 114.

7. Strachey, *Standard Edition*, 22: 115.

8. Strachey, *Standard Edition*, 22:131.

9. Strachey, *Standard Edition*, 19: 33.

10. Strachey, *Standard Edition*, 19: 258.

11. Strachey, *Standard Edition*, 20:38.

12. Strachey, *Standard Edition*, 7: 150.

13. Strachey, *Standard Edition*, 7: 138–39.

14. Strachey, *Standard Edition*, 23: 188.

15. Strachey, *Standard Edition*, 21: 104.

16. Strachey, *Standard Edition*, 7: 198.

17. Strachey, *Standard Edition*, 21: 106.

18. Strachey, *Standard Edition*, 7: 222.

19. Strachey, *Standard Edition*, 4: 197.

20. Strachey, *Standard Edition*, 19: 179.

21. Strachey, *Standard Edition*, 20: 318

22. Lucy Bland, "Trial by Sexology?: Maud Allan, Salome and the "Cult of the Clitoris' Case," in Lucy Bland and Laura Doan, eds, *Sexology in Culture: Labelling Bodies and Desires* (Chicago: University of Chicago Press, 1998), 195.

23. 18. Strachey, *Standard Edition*, 16: 318.

24. Elisabeth A. Lloyd, *The Case of the Female Orgasm: Bias in the Science of Evolution* (Cambridge: Harvard University Press, 2005).

Chapter 10

1. www:americanrhetoric.com/speeches/barackobama/barackobamaweekly-transition7.htm.

2. Michel Foucault, "On Literature," *Foucault Live* (New York: Semiotexte, 1989), 150.

3. A . J. Froude, *Essays in Historical Criticism* (New York: Scribners, 1901), 295.

4. John Burroughs, "Science and Literature," *The Writings of John Burroughs* (New York: Houghton Mifflin, 1905), 8: 51.

5. Burroughs, "Science and Literature," 51.

6. Burroughs, "Science and Literature," 54.

7. Burroughs, "Science and Literature," 64.

8. Burroughs, "Science and Literature," 70.

9. Burroughs, "Science and Literature," 74.

Index